The Soul of Dem

Edward Howard Griggs

Alpha Editions

This edition published in 2024

ISBN : 9789357960823

Design and Setting By
Alpha Editions
www.alphaedis.com
Email - info@alphaedis.com

I

THE WORLD TRAGEDY

We are living under the shadow of the greatest world tragedy in the history of mankind. Not even the overthrow of the old Roman empire was so colossal a disaster as this. Inevitably we are bewildered by it. Utterly unanticipated, at least in its world extent, for we had believed mankind too far advanced for such a chaos of brute force to recur, it overwhelms our vision. Man had been going forward steadily, inventing and discovering, until in the last hundred years his whole world had been transformed. Suddenly the entire range of invention is turned against Man. The machinery of comfort and progress becomes the enginery of devastation. Under such a shock, we ask, "Has civilization over-reached itself? Has the machine run away with its maker?" The imagination is staggered. We are too much in the storm to see across the storm.

When the War began, it was over our minds as a dark cloud. It was the last conscious thought as we went to sleep at night, and the first to which we awakened in the morning: wakening with a dumb sense of something wrong, as if we had suffered a personal tragedy, and then as we came to clear consciousness we said, "O yes, the War!" The days have passed into weeks, the weeks into months and years: inevitably we become benumbed to the long continued disaster. It is impossible to think deaths and mutilations in terms of millions. Even those who stand in the immediate presence of it and suffer most terribly become calloused to it: much more must we who stood so long apart and have not yet felt the brunt of it. Even our entrance into the whirling vortex, drawing ever nearer our shores, has failed to waken us to a realizing sense of it. Nevertheless, these years through which we are now living are the most important in the entire history of the world. It is probable that the future will look back upon them as the years determining the destiny of mankind for ages to come.

How this terrible fact of War falls across all philosophies! Complacent optimisms, so widely current recently, are put out of court by it. The pleasant interpretations mediocrity formulates of the universe are torn to tatters. There is at least the refreshment of standing face to face with brute actuality, though it crash all our "little systems" to the ground. Philosophy must wait. The interpretations cannot be hastened, while the facts are multiplying with such bewildering rapidity. The one certainty is that an entirely new world is being born—*what* it will be, no one knows.

Nevertheless, we have gone far enough to recognize that all our thinking will be transformed under the influence of the struggle. It will be impossible for us, after the War, to do what we have done so widely hitherto: proclaim one range of ethical ideals and standards, and live to something widely different in practice. Either we shall have to abandon the standards, or bring our conduct measurably into harmony with them. We shall be unable longer to hold unconsciously in solution Christianity and the gospel of brute force. One or the other must be rejected, or both consciously reconstructed. The effect on the thought life of the world will be even greater—vastly greater—than that of the French Revolution. The twentieth century will differ from the nineteenth more than that did from the eighteenth. The effect on the relations of different social groups throughout the world will be so far-reaching that possibly the democracy and socialism of the nineteenth century may look like remote historic phenomena, such as the Athenian tribal system or mediaeval feudalism.

Thus our whole social philosophy will have to be remolded. We Americans are still in the patent medicine period of politics, trusting to political devices on the surface for the cure of any evils that arise. All across the country, like an epidemic of disease has gone the notion —if anything is the matter with us, just pass another law. Thus we are suffering under an ill-considered mass of legislation, while blindly trusting to it to solve all problems. Legislation is no solution for moral evils. It is possible, to some extent, to suppress vice by legislation, but not to create virtue. Virtue can be developed only by conduct and education. You cannot drive men into the kingdom of heaven with the whip of legislation; and if you could, you would so change the atmosphere of the place that one would prefer to take the other road.

If our democracy is to survive, we must think it through; carrying it down, from these superficial political devices, into our industry and commerce, still so largely dominated by feudal ideas of the middle age, into our science and art, far more completely into our education, into our social relationship, and beyond all else, into our fundamental attitude of mind. Democracy is, at bottom, not a series of political forms, but a way of life.

Thus the War will be the supreme test of democracy. The question it will settle is this: can free men, by voluntary cooperation, develop an efficiency and an endurance which will make it possible for them to stand and protect their liberties against the machinery and aggressive ambitions of autocratic empires where everything is done paternally from the top? If they can, then democracy will survive and grow as the highest form of society for ages to come; if not, then democracy will pass and be succeeded by some other social order.

That is why this War has been our war from the beginning, though we have entered it so late. As we look back upon the struggle of Athens and the other free Greek cities with the overwhelming hordes of Asia, at Marathon and Salamis, as the conflict that saved democracy for Europe and made possible the civilization of the Occident, so it is probable that the world will look back upon this colossal War as the same struggle, multiplied a thousand times in the men and munitions employed, the struggle determining the future of democracy and civilization for generations, perhaps for all time.

II

THE CONFLICT OF IDEAS IN THE WAR

The world has been confused as to the issue in this War, because of the multitude of its causes and of the antagonisms it involves; yet under all the national and racial hatreds, the economic jealousies, certain great ideas are being tested out.

Apologists for Germany have told us, even with pride, that in Germany the supreme conception is the dedication of Man to the State. This was not true of old Germany. Before the formation of the Prussian empire, her spirit was intensely individualistic. She stood preeminently for freedom of thought and action. It was this that gave her noble spiritual heritage. Goethe is the most individualistic of world masters. Froebel developed, in the Kindergarten, one of the purest of democracies. Luther and German protestantism represented the affirmation of individual conscience as against hierarchical control. It was this spirit that gave Germany her golden age of literature, her unmatched group of spiritual philosophers, her religious teachers, her pre-eminence in music.

Nevertheless, the Prussian state, autocratic from its inception, received philosophic justification in a series of thinkers, culminating in Hegel, who regarded the individual as a capricious egotist, the state, incarnate in its sovereign, as the supreme spiritual entity. He justified war, regarding it as a permanent necessity, and practically made might, right, in arguing that a conquering nation is justified by its more fruitful idea in annexing the weaker, while the conquered, in being conquered, is judged of God. Here is the philosophic justification of that Prussian arrogance which in Nietzsche is carried into glittering rhetoric. Thus the Prussian state from afar back was opposed to the general spirit of old Germany.

Since 1870, it must be admitted, that spirit is gone. With the formation of the Prussian empire and for the half century of its existence, every force of social control—press, church, state, education, social opinion—was deliberately employed to stamp on the German people one idea—the subordination of the individual to the state, as the supreme and only virtue. How far has the policy succeeded? Apparently absolutely. To the outside observer the old spirit seems utterly gone. How far this policy has been helped by the cultivation of the fear of the Slav, one cannot say. Looking at the map of Europe, one sees that the geographical relation of Germany to the great Slavic empire is not unlike the relation of Holland to Germany.

Thus the deliberate fostering of fear of the vast empire of the East has done much to strengthen the hands of the Prussian regime in its chosen task.

Nevertheless, when one recalls the spiritual heritage of Germany: when one thinks of Herder, Schiller and Goethe; Tauler, Luther and Schleiermacher; Froebel, Herbart and Richter; Kant, Fichte and Novalis; Mozart, Beethoven and Wagner; one feels that something of the old German heritage must survive. When the German people find out what has happened to them and why, that heritage surely ought to show in some reaction against the present autocratic regime, after the War closes, if not before, perhaps even to the extent of making Germany a republic. That would be some compensation for the waste and destruction of the War. Meantime Germany stands now, ruthlessly, for the dedication of Man to the State.

One can understand why a Prussian minister forbade the teaching of Froebel's ideas in Prussia during the latter period of the educator's life. So one understands the hatred of Goethe because he refused allegiance to a narrow nationalism and remained cosmopolitan in his world-view. Similarly Hegel, with his justification of absolute monarchy and his theory of the German state as the acme of all spiritual evolution, was the acclaimed orthodox philosopher of Prussia, while the individualist, Schopenhauer, was neglected and despised.

One must have lived in Germany to realize the absolute control of the State over the individual—the incessant surveillance, the petty regulations, the constant interference with private life. It was to escape just this vexatious control, with the arduous militarism in which it culminates, that so vast a multitude of Germans left their native land and came to the United States—not all of whom have shown appreciation and loyalty to the free land that welcomed them.

III

THE IDEAS FOR WHICH THE ALLIED NATIONS FIGHT

In contrast to the idea for which Germany now stands, the Anglo-Saxon instinctively and tenaciously believes in the liberty and initiative of the individual. We, of course, are no longer Anglo-Saxon. When De Tocqueville in 1831 visited our country, surveyed our institutions and, after returning home, made his trenchant diagnosis of our democracy, he could justly designate us Anglo-Americans. That time is past; we are to-day everything and nothing: a great nation in the womb of time, struggling to be born.

Nevertheless, Anglo-American ideas still dominate and inspire our civilization. It is, indeed, remarkable to what an extent this is true, in the face of the mingling of heterogeneous races in our population. As English is our speech, so Anglo-American ideas are still the soul of our life and institutions.

This is evident in the jealousy of authority. We resent the intrusion of the government into affairs of private life, and prefer to submit to annoyances and even injustice on the part of other individuals, rather than to have protection at the price of paternalistic regulation by the state. We resent any law that we do not see is necessary to the general welfare, and are rather lawless even then. This shows clearly in our reaction on legislation in regard to drink. The prohibition of intoxicating liquor is about the surest way to make an Anglo-Saxon want to go out and get drunk, even when he has no other inclination in that direction. In Boston, under the eleven o'clock closing law, men in public restaurants will at times order, at ten minutes of eleven, eight or ten glasses of beer or whiskey, for fear they might want them, whereas, if the restriction had not been present, two or three would have sufficed.

Not long ago we saw the very labor leaders who forced the Adamson law through congress, threatening to disobey any legislation limiting their own freedom of action, even though vitally necessary to the freedom of all.

The general behavior under automobile and traffic regulation illustrates the tendency evenmore clearly. Thinking over the list of acquaintances who own automobiles, one finds it hard to recall one who would not break the speed law at a convenient opportunity. Even a staid college professor, who has walked the walled-in path all his life: let him get a Ford runabout, and in three months he is exultant in running as close as possible to every foot traveler and in exceeding the speed limit at any favorable chance. These are not beautiful expressions of our national spirit, but they serve to illustrate our instinctive individualism.

Especially are we jealous of highly centralized authority. De Tocqueville argued that we would never be able to develop a strong central government, and that our democracy would be menaced with failure by that lack. That his prophecy has proved false and our federal government has become so strong is due only to the accidents of our history and the exigency of the tremendous problems we have had to solve.

The same individualistic spirit is strong in England. It has been particularly evident, during the War, in the resentment of military authority as applied to labor conditions. The artisans and their leaders dreaded to give up liberties for which they had struggled through generations, for fear that those rights would not be readily accorded them again after the War. It must be admitted that this fear is justified. The same spirit was evident in the fight on conscription. This attitude has been a handicap to England in successfully carrying on the War, as it is to us; but it shows how strong is the essential spirit of democracy in both lands.

In France, the Revolution was at bottom an affirmation of individualism — of the right of the people, as against classes and kings, to seek life, liberty and happiness. The great words, *Liberty, Equality, Fraternity*, that the French placed upon their public buildings in the period of the Revolution, are the essential battle-cry of true democracy,—as it is to be, rather than as it is at present.

Through her peculiar situation, threatened and overshadowed by potential enemies, France has been forced to a policy of militarism, with a large subordination of the individual to the state. The subordination, however, is voluntary. That is touchingly evident in the beautiful fraternization of French officers and men in the present War. With our Anglo-Saxon reserve, we smile at the pictures of grave generals kissing bearded soldiers, in recognition of valor, but it is a significant expression of the voluntary equality and brotherhood of Frenchmen in this War. The reason France has risen with such splendid courage and unity is the consciousness of every Frenchman that complete defeat in this War would mean that there would be no France in the future, that Paris would be a larger Strassburg, and France a greater Alsace-Lorraine. While the subordination has been thus voluntary, surely the French soldiers, man for man, have proved themselves the equal of any soldiers on earth.

The anomaly of the first two years of the War was the presence of the vast Russian autocratic empire on the side of the allied democracies. For Russia, however, the War was of the people, rather than of the autocracy at the top, and one saw that Russia would emerge from the War changed and purified. What one could not foresee was that, under the awakening of the people, Russia could pass, in a day, through a Revolution as profound in its character and consequences as the great explosion in France. It would be almost a miracle if so complete a Revolution, in such a vast, benighted empire, were not followed by decades of recurrent chaos and anarchy. If Russia avoids this fate, she will present a unique experience in history. The tendency to abrogate all authority, the spectacle of regiments of soldiers becoming debating societies to discuss whether or not they shall obey orders and fight, are ominous signs for the next period. Emancipated Russia must learn, if necessary through bitter suffering, that liberty is not license, that democracy is not anarchy, but voluntary and intelligent obedience to just laws and the chosen executors of those laws. Meantime, whatever her immediate future may be, Russia's transformation has clarified the issue and justified her place with the allied democracies. However long and confused her struggle, there can be no return to the past, and, in the end, her Revolution means democracy.

Thus, in democracy, the State exists for Man. Other forms of society seek the interest or welfare of an individual, a group or a class, democracy aims at the welfare, that is, the liberty, happiness, growth, intelligence, helpfulness of *all the people*. Under all the welter of this world struggle, it is therefore these great contrasting ideas that are being tested out, perhaps for all time. What is their relative value for efficiency, initiative, invention, endurance, permanence; beneath all, what is their final value for the happiness and helpfulness of all human beings?

IV

MORAL STANDARDS AND THE MORAL ORDER

There is only one moral order of the universe—one range of moral as of physical law. For instance, the law of gravitation—simplest of physical principles—holds the last star in the abyss of space, rounds the dew-drop on the petal of a spring violet and determines the symmetry of living organisms; but it is one and unchanging, a fundamental pull in the nature of matter itself. So with moral laws: they are not superadded to life by some divine or other authority. They are simply the fundamental principles in the nature of life itself, which we must obey to grow and be happy.

If the moral order is one and unchanging, man does change in relation to it, and moral standards are relative to the stage of his growth. History is filled with illustrations of this relativity of ethical standards.

For instance: human slavery doubtless began as an act of beneficence on the part of some philanthropist well in advance of his age. The first man who, in the dim dawn of history, said to the captive he had made in war, "I will not kill you and eat you; I will let you live and work for me the rest of your life": that man instituted human slavery; but it was distinctly a step upward, from something that had been far worse.

Homer represents Ulysses as the favorite pupil of Pallas Athena, goddess of wisdom: why? Baldly stated, because Ulysses was the shrewdest and most successful liar in classic antiquity. If Ulysses were to appear in a society of decent men to-day, he would be excluded from their companionship, and for the same reason that led Homer to glorify him as the favorite pupil of the goddess of wisdom. Thus what is a virtue at one stage of development becomes a vice as man climbs to higher recognition of the moral order.

Just because the moral standard is relative, it is absolutely binding where it applies. In other words, if you see the light shining on your path, you owe obedience to the light; one who does not see it, does not owe obedience in the same way. If you do not obey your light, your punishment is that you lose the light—degenerate to a lower plane, and it is the worst punishment imaginable.

Thus the same act may be for the undeveloped life, non-moral, for the developed, distinctly immoral. Before the instincts of personal modesty and purity were developed, careless sex-promiscuity meant something entirely different from what a descent to it means in our society. When a man of some primitive tribe went out and killed a man of another tribe, the action was totally different morally from .the murder by a man of one community of a citizen of a neighboring town to-day.

This gradual elevation of moral standards, or growth in the recognition of the sacredness of life and the obligation to other individuals, can be traced historically as a long and confused process. There was a time, in the remote past, when no law was recognized except that of the strong arm. The man who wanted anything, took it, if he was strong enough, and others submitted to his superior force. Then follows an age when the family is the supreme social unit. Each member of the family group feels the pain or pleasure of all the others as something like his own, but all outside this circle are as the beasts. This is the condition among the Veddahs of Ceylon, studied so interestingly by Haeckel. Living in isolated family groups, scattered through the tropical wilderness: one man, one woman and their children forming the social unit: they as nearly represent primitive life as any other body of people now on the earth.

Then follows a long roll of ages when the tribe is the highest social unit. Each member of the tribe is conscious of the sacredness of life of all the other members and of some obligation toward them; but men of other tribes may be slain as freely as the beasts. Then comes a period when appreciation of the sacredness of life is extended over all those of the same race, tested generally by their speaking somewhat the same language. That was the condition in classic antiquity: it was "Jew and Gentile," "Greek and barbarian"—the very word "barbarous" coming from the unintelligible sounds, to the Greeks, of those who spoke other than the Hellenic tongue. Even Plato, with all his far-sighted humanism, says, in the *Republic*, that in the ideal state, "Greeks should deal with barbarians as Greeks now deal with one another." If one remembers what occurred in the Peloponnesian war—how Greek men voted to kill all the men of military age in a conquered Greek city and sell all the women and children into slavery—one will see that Plato's dream of humanity was not so very wide.

From that time on, there has been further extension of the appreciation of the sacredness of life and of the consciousness of moral obligation toward other human beings. We are far from the end of the path. Our sympathies are still limited by accidents of time and place, race and color; but we have gone far enough to see what the end would be, were we to reach it: a sympathy so wide, an appreciation of the sacredness of life so universal, that each of us would feel the joy or sorrow of every other human being, alive to-day or to be alive to-morrow, as something like his own. Moreover, in all civilized society, we have gone far enough to renounce the right to private vengeance and adjustment of quarrels: we live under established courts of law, with organized civil force to carry out their judgments. This gives relative peace and security, and a general, if imperfect, application of the moral law.

V

THE PRESENT STATE OF INTERNATIONAL RELATIONS

The astounding anomaly of modern civilization is the way we have lagged behind in applying to groups and nations of men the moral laws, universally recognized as binding over individuals. For instance, about twenty years ago we coined and used widely the phrase, "soulless corporation," to designate our great combinations of capital in industry and commerce. Why was that phrase used so widely? The answer is illuminating: we took it for granted that an individual employer would treat his artisans to some extent as human beings and not merely as cog-wheels in a productive machine; but we also took it for granted that an impersonal corporation, where no individual was dominantly responsible, would regard its artisans merely as pieces of machinery, with no respect whatever for their humanity.

The supreme paradox, however, is in the relation of nations: it is there that we have most amazingly lagged behind in applying the moral laws universally accepted in the relations of individuals. For instance, long before this War began we heard it proclaimed, even proudly, by certain philosophers, in more than one nation, that the state is the supreme spiritual unit, that there is no law higher than its interest, that the state makes the law and may break it at will. When a great statesman in Germany, doubtless in a moment of intense anger and irritation, used the phrase that has gone all across the earth, "*scrap of paper,*" for a sacred treaty between nations, he was only making a pungent practical application of the philosophy in question.

Do we regard self-preservation as the highest law for the individual? Distinctly not. Here is a crowded theater and a sudden cry of fire, with the ensuing panic: if strong men trample down and kill women and children, in the effort to save their own lives, we regard them with loathing and contempt. On the other hand, it is just this plea of national self-preservation that the German regime has used in cynical justification of its every atrocity—the initial violation of Belgium, the making war ruthlessly on civil populations, the atrocious spying and plotting in the bosom of neutral and friendly nations, the destruction of monuments of art and devastation of the cities, fields, orchards and forests of northern France, and finally the submarine warfare on the world's shipping. No civilized human being would, for a moment, think of using the plea of self-preservation to justify comparable conduct in individual life.

Consider international diplomacy: much of it has been merely shrewd and skillful lying. If you will review the list of the most famous diplomats of Europe for the last thousand years, you will find that a considerable portion of them won their fame and reputation by being a little more shrewd and successful liars than the diplomats with whom they had to deal in other lands. In other words, their conduct has been exactly on the plane that Ulysses represented in personal life, afar back in classic antiquity.

Take an illustration a little nearer home. If you were doing business on one side of the street and had two competitors in the same line, across the way, and a cyclone swept the town, destroying their establishments and sparing yours: you, as an individual, would be ashamed to take advantage of the disaster under which your rivals were suffering, using the time while they were out of business to lure their customers away from them and bind those customers to you so securely that your competitors would never be able to get them back. You would scorn such conduct as an individual; but when it comes to a relation of the nations: during the first two years of the War, from the highest government circles down to the smallest country newspaper, we were urged to take advantage of the disaster under which our European rivals were suffering, win their international customers away from them and bind those customers to us so securely that Europe would never be able to get them back. Not that we were urged to industry and enterprise—that is always right—but actually to seek to profit by the sufferings of others—conduct we would regard as utterly unworthy in personal life.

If your neighbor were to say, "My personal aspirations demand this portion of your front yard," and he were to attempt to fence it in: the situation is unimaginable; but when a nation says, "My national aspirations demand this portion of your territory," and proceeds to annex it: if the nation is strong enough to carry it out, a large part of the world acquiesces.

The relations of nations are thus still largely on the plane of primitive life among individuals, or, since nations are made up of civilized and semi-civilized persons, it would be fairer to say that the relations of nations are comparable to those prevailing among individuals when a group of men goes far out from civil society, to the frontier, beyond the reach of courts of law and their police forces: then nearly always there is a reversion to the rule of the strong arm. That is what Kipling meant in exclaiming,

"There's never a law of God or man runs north of fifty-three."

That condition prevailed all across our frontier in the early days. For instance, the cattle men came, pasturing their herds on the hills and plains, using the great expanse of land not yet taken up by private ownership. A little later came the sheep men, with vast flocks of sheep, which nibbled every blade of grass and other edible plant down to the ground, thus starving out the cattle. What followed? The cattle men got together by night, rode down the sheep-herders, shot them or drove them out, or were themselves driven out.

So on the frontier, in the early days, a weakling staked out an agricultural or mining claim. A ruffian appears, who is a sure shot, jumps the claim and drives the other out. It was the rule of the strong arm, and it was evident on the frontier all across the country.

This is exactly the state that a considerable part of the world has reached in international relationship to-day. Claim-jumping is still accepted and widely practised among the nations. That is, in fact, the way in which all empires have been built—by a succession of successful claim-jumpings. Consider the most impressive of them all, the old Roman empire. Rome was a city near the mouth of the Tiber. She reached out and conquered a few neighboring cities in the Latin plain, binding them securely to herself by domestic and economic ties. Then she extended her power south and north, crossed into northern Africa, conquered Gaul and Spain, swept Asia Minor, until a territory three thousand by two thousand miles in extent was under the sway of her all-conquering arm.

What justified Rome, as far as she had justification, was the remarkable strength and wisdom with which she established law and order and the protections of civil society over all the conquered territory, until often the subject populations were glad they had come under the all-dominant sway of Rome, since their situation was so much more peaceful and happy than before. Such justification, however, is after the fact: it is not moral justification of the building of the empire. That represented a succession of claim-jumpings.

For an illustration from more modern history, take the greatest international crime of the last five hundred years, with one exception— the partition of Poland. It is true the Polish nobles were a nuisance to their neighbors, ever quarreling among themselves, with no central authority powerful enough to restrain them, but that did not justify the action taken. Three nations, or rather the autocratic sovereigns of those nations, powerful enough to accomplish the crime, agreed to partition Poland among themselves. They did it, with the result that there are plenty of Poles in the world to-day, but there is no Poland.

Consider the possession of Silesia by Prussia. Silesia was an integral part of the Austrian domain, long so recognized. Friedrich the Great wanted it. He annexed it. The deed caused him many years of recurring, devastating wars; again and again he was near the point of utter defeat; but he succeeded in bringing the war to a successful conclusion, and Silesia is part of Prussia today. The strong arm conquest is the only reason.

So is it with Germany's possession of Schleswig-Holstein, with Austria in Herzegovina and Bosnia, France in Algiers, Italy in Tripoli: they are all instances of claim-jumping, reprehensible in varying degrees.

I suppose no thoughtful Englishman would attempt to justify, on high moral grounds, the building up of the British empire: for instance, the possession of Egypt and India by Britain. How does India happen to be a part of the British realm? Every one knows the answer. The East India Company was simply the most adventurous and enterprising trading company then in the world. It grew rich trading with the Orient, established the supremacy of the British merchant marine, got into difficulties with French rivals and native rulers, fought brilliantly for its rights, as it had every reason to do, conquered territory and consolidated its possessions, ruling chiefly through native princes. It became so powerful that it did not seem wise to the British government to permit a private corporation to exercise such ever-growing political authority. It was regulated, and in the end abolished, by act of Parliament; its possessions were taken over by the Crown; the conquests were extended and completed, and India today is a gem in the crown of the British empire.

What justifies Britain, as far as she has justification, is the remarkable wisdom and generosity with which she has extended, not onlylaw and order and protection to life and property, but freedom and autonomous self-government, to her colonies and subject populations, with certain tragic exceptions, about as fast as this could safely be done. It is that which holds the British empire together. Great irregular empire, stretching over a large part of the globe: but for this it would fall to pieces over night. It would be impossible for force, administered at the top, to hold it together. The splendid response of her colonies in this War has been purely voluntary. That Canada has four hundred thousand trained men at the front, or ready to go, is due wholly to her free response to the wise generosity of England's policy, and in no degree to compulsion, which would have been impossible. This justification of the British empire is, nevertheless, as in the case of Rome, after the fact, and does not justify morally the building up of the empire.

Our own hands are not entirely clean. It is true we came late on the stage of history, and, starting as a democracy, were instinctively opposed to empire building. Thus our brief record is cleaner than that of the older nations. Nevertheless, there are examples of claim-jumping in our history. The most tragic of all is a large part of our treatment of the American Indians. It is true, with Anglo-Saxon hypocrisy, we tried to make every steal a bargain.

Many an expanse of territory has been bought with a jug of rum. The Indian knew nothing about the ownership of land; we did. So we made the deed, and he accepted it. Then, to his surprise, he found he had to move off from land where for generations his ancestors had hunted and fought, with no idea of private ownership. So we pushed him on and on. Of late decades we have become ashamed, tried in awkward fashion to render some compensation for the wrongs done, but the larger part of the story is sad indeed.

There is, of course, another side to all this: the more highly developed nations do owe leadership and service in helping those below to climb the path of civilization; but let one answer fairly how much of empire building has been due to this altruistic spirit, and how much to selfishness and the lust for power and possession.

VI

THE ETHICS OF INTERNATIONAL RELATIONSHIP

We have seen that all empires have been built up by a series of successful aggressions, and that claim-jumping still characterizes the relations of the nations. Nevertheless, there has been some progress in applying to groups and nations the moral principles we recognize as binding upon individuals. Consider again our internal life: it was twenty years ago that we coined and used so widely the phrase "soulless corporations" for our great combinations of capital in industry. To-day that phrase is rarely heard. One sees it seldom even in the pages of surviving "muck-raking" magazines. Why has a phrase, used so widely in the past, all but disappeared? Again the answer is illuminating: there has been tremendous growth in twenty years, on the part of our great corporations, in treating their employees as human beings and not merely as cog-wheels in a productive machine. When the greatest corporation in the United States voluntarily raises the wages of all its employees in the country ten per cent., five several times, within a few months, as the Steel trust has recently done, something has happened. It may be said, "they did it because it was good business": twenty years ago they would not have recognized that it was good business. It may be said, "they did it to avoid strikes": twenty years ago they would have welcomed the strikes, fought them through and gained what selfish advantage was possible. The point is, there has been vast increase in the consciousness of moral responsibility on the part of corporations toward their artisans. This has been due partly to legislation, but mainly to education and the awakening of public conscience. If you wish to find the greatest arrogance and selfishness now, you will discover it, not among the capitalists: they are timid and submissive—strangely so. You will find it rather in certain leaders of the labor movement, with their consciousness of newly-gained powers.

Some growth there has been in the application of the same moral principles even to the relations of the nations. For instance: a hundred years ago the Napoleonic wars had just come to an end. In the days of Napoleon men generally gloried in war; to-day most of them bitterly regret it, and fight because they believe they are fighting for high moral aims or for national self-preservation, whether they are right or wrong.

When Napoleon conquered a country, often he pushed the weakling king off the throne, and replaced him with a member of his own family—at times a worse weakling. Think of such a thing being attempted to-day: it is unimaginable, unless the worst tyranny on earth got the upper hand for the next three hundred years of human history.

A more pungent illustration of progress is the feverish desire, shown by each of the combatants in this world struggle, to prove that he did not begin it. Now some one began it. A hundred years ago belligerents would not have been so anxious to prove their innocence: then victory closed all accounts and no one went behind the returns. The feverish anxiety each combatant has shown to establish his innocence of initiating this devastating War is conclusive proof that even the worst of them recognizes that they all must finally stand before the moral court of the world's conscience and be judged. The same tendency is shown in the efforts of Germany—grotesquely and tragically sophistical as they are— to justify her ever-expanding, freshly-invented atrocities. At least she is aware that they require justification.

This explains why we react so bitterly even on what would have been accepted a century ago. What was taken for granted yesterday is not tolerated to-day, and what is taken for granted to-day will not be tolerated in a to-morrow that maybe is not so distant as in our darker moments we imagine.

What would be the conclusion of this process? It would be, would it not, the complete application to the relations of the nations, of the moral principles universally accepted as binding upon individuals? If it is true that the moral order of the universe is one and unchanging, then *what is right for a man is right for a nation of men, and what is wrong for a man is wrong for a nation*; and no fallacious reasoning should be allowed to blind us to that basic truth.

This would mean the end of all diplomacy of lying and deceit. The relations of the nations would be placed on the same plane of relative honesty and frankness now prevailing among individuals: not absolute truth—few of us practice that—but that general ability to trust each other, in word and conduct, that is the foundation of our business and social life.

It would mean the end of empire building. Those empires that exist would fall naturally into their component parts. If those parts remained affiliated with the central government, it would be only through the voluntary choice of the majority of the population dwelling upon the territory. Thus every people would be affiliated with the government to which it naturally belonged and with which it wished to be affiliated.

It would mean finally a voluntary federation of the nations, with the establishment of a world court of justice; but no weak-kneed, spineless arbitration court: rather a court of justice, comparable to those established over individuals, whose judgments would be enforced by an international military and naval police, contributed by the federated nations.

People misunderstand this proposal. They imagine it would mean the giving over of the entire military and naval equipment of each federated nation to the central court. Far from it: each nation would retain, for defense purposes, the mass of its manhood and the larger fraction of its limited equipment, while a minor fraction would be contributed to the world court.

When this is achieved there will be, for the first time in the history of the world, the dawn of the longed-for era of universal and relatively permanent peace for mankind.

It is a far-off dream, is it not? Let us admit it frankly, and it seems further off than it did four years ago; for the approximations to it, achieved through international law, we have seen go down in a blind welter, through the invention of new instruments of destruction and the willful perpetration of illegal and immoral atrocities in this horrible War.

Nevertheless, it is not so far off as in ourdarker moments we fear. If this world War ends justly; which means if it ends so that the people dwelling on any territory are affiliated with the government to which they naturally belong and with which they wish to be affiliated, the dream will be brought appreciably nearer. If the War ends unjustly, which means if it ends with the gratification of the ambitions of aggressive tyranny, the dream will be put remotely far off. If a peace is patched up meantime, with no solution, it will mean Europe sleeping on its arms, and the breaking out of the war with multiplied devastation within twenty years. That is why these blithely undertaken peace missions and other efforts at peace without victory, even when not cloaks for pro-German movements, are such preposterous absurdities or else play directly into the hands of tyranny.

At best, however, the dream is a long way ahead. Men dislike to give up power, nations equally. It will take a long process of international moral education to induce the nations to renounce their arbitrary powers, their right to adjust all their own quarrels, and lead them to enter voluntarily a federation under a world court of Justice. This, nevertheless, is the hope of the world, toward which we should work with all our might.

VII

AMERICA'S DUTY IN INTERNATIONAL RELATIONS

Since the world solution is, at best, so remote, our question is: what are we to do meantime? Our entrance into the War partially answers the question. We have before us the immediate task of aiding in overthrowing autocracy and tyranny and of defending our liberties and those of the nations that stand for democracy. This is the first duty, but not the only one.

More definitely than any other nation we have thrown down to the world the challenge of democracy. We have said, "Away with kings, we will have no more of them! Away with castes and ruling classes, we will have no more of them!" As a matter of fact, democracies have no rulers—the word survives from an older order of society—they have guides, leaders and representatives. If you wish to use the word, in a democracy every man is the ruler—and every woman too, we hope, before long. To this ideal we are committed and it carries certain obligations; for every right carries a duty, and every duty, a right. Often the best way to get a privilege is by assuming a responsibility. That is a truth it would be well for the leaders of the feminist and labor movements to recognize. The obligations carried by the challenge of our democracy are clear.

We Americans should have done, once and for all time, with the diplomacy of lying and deceit. Fortunately our recent traditions are in harmony with this demand; but we should not depend upon the happy accident of an administration which takes the right attitude. It should be the open and universal demand of the American people that those who represent us shall place the relations we sustain to other nations permanently on the same plane of frank honesty, generally prevailing among individuals. Incidentally, any politician or statesman who, at this heart-breaking crisis of the world's life, dares play party politics with our international relations, should be damned forever by the vote of the American people.

Further, it is our duty to have done with all dream of empire building. It is not for us: let us abandon it frankly and forever. Those dependencies which have come to us through the accidents of our history should be granted autonomous self-government at the earliest moment at which they can safely take it over—which does not necessarily mean to-morrow. If they remain affiliated with us it should be only through the voluntary choice of the majority of the population dwelling upon them.

It is, moreover, our duty to lead the world in the effort to form a federation of the nations and establish the aforesaid world court of justice, with the international military and naval police to enforce its judgments.

More than this is demanded: on the basis of the challenge of our democracy, it is our duty to rise to the point of placing justice higher than commercial interest. It is a hard demand; but, with the latent idealism in our American life, surely we can rise to it. For instance, the vexed puzzle of the tariff will never be justly and permanently settled, till it is settled primarily as a problem of moral international relationship, and not as one merely of economic interest and advantage.

For example, a tariff wall between the United States and Canada is as preposterous an absurdity as would be a long line of bristling fortifications along the three thousand and more miles of international boundary. We are not protecting ourselves from slave labor over there. They are not protecting themselves from slave labor here. Barring a few lines of industry, there are the same conditions of labor, production and distribution both sides of the line. The only reason for a tariff wall is their wish, or our wish, or the wish of each, to gain some advantage at the expense of the other party. Now every business man knows that any trade that benefits one and injures the other party to it is bad business, as well as bad ethics, in the long run. Good business benefits both traders all the time.

On the other hand, when it comes to protecting our labor from competition with slave labor in other quarters of the earth, we have not only the right, but the duty to do it. So when it is a matter of protecting our industries from being swamped by the unloading of vast quantities of goods, produced under the feverish and abnormal conditions, sure to prevail in Europe after the War, we have again, not only the right, but the duty to do it.

Finally, a still higher call is upon us: we must somehow rise to the point of placing humanity above the nation. It is true, "Charity begins at home," certainly justice should. One should educate one's own children, before worrying over the children of the neighborhood; clean up one's own town, before troubling about the city further away. Often the whole is helped best by serving the part; but it is with national patriotism as it is with family affection. The latter is a lovely quality and the source of much that is best in the world; but when family affection is an instrument for gaining special privilege at the expense of the good of society, a means of attaining debauching luxury and selfish aggrandisement, it is an abomination. The man who prays God's blessing on himself, his wife and his children, and nobody else, is a mean man, and he never gets blessed—not from God. Similarly, the man who seeks the interest of his own nation, against the welfare of mankind, who prays God's blessing only on his own people, is equally a mean man, and his prayer, also, is never answered from the Most High. The world has advanced too far for the spirit of a narrow nationalism. The recrudescence of such a spirit is one of the sad consequences of this world War. Only in a spirit of international brotherhood, in dedication to the welfare of humanity, can democracy go towards its goal.

These are the obligations following upon the challenge of democracy we have proclaimed to the nations.

VIII

THE GOSPEL AND THE SUPERSTITION OF NON-RESISTANCE

The first condition of fulfilling the responsibilities imposed upon us by the challenge of our democracy is, now and hereafter, readiness and willingness for self-respecting self-defense, defense of our liberties and of the principles and ideals for which we stand. There is much nonsense talked about non-resistance to evil. It is a lovely thing in certain high places of the moral life. It was well that Socrates remained in the common criminal prison in Athens and drank the hemlock poison; but nine times out of ten it would have been better to run away, as he had an opportunity to do. It was good that Jesus healed the ear of the servant of the high priest,—and good that St. Peter cut it off.

In other words, acts of non-resistance and self-sacrifice are fine flowers of the moral life; but you cannot have flowers unless their roots are below ground, otherwise they quickly wither. Thus, to have sound value, these acts of non-resistance and self-sacrifice must rest on a solid foundation of self-affirmation and resistance to evil.

As with the individual, so with the nation: there come high moments in a nation's life, when a strong people might resist and deliberately chooses not to. As an illustration, take our Mexican problem. The announcement that under no circumstances would we intervene, may have led to misunderstanding. Our purpose to let the Mexican people work out their own problem may have been taken to mean that we would not justly protect ourselves, with consequent encouragement to border raiding. Nevertheless, if there has been any error in handling the situation, it has been on the better side—on the side of patience, generosity, long-suffering, giving the other fellow another chance, and another and another, even though he does not deserve them. Now that is not the side on which human nature usually errs. The common temptation is to selfishness and unjust aggression. Since that is the case, if we cannot strike the just balance, it is better to push too far on the other side and avoid the common mistake.

Suppose, after the War, Japan, alone or in conjunction with one or another European power, closes the door to China: one can imagine circumstances where we, with the right to insist that the door be kept open, and perhaps, by that time, something of the strength to enforce that right, might deliberately say, "No, we will not resist." Not that, with our present situation, such action is desirable, but that one can imagine conditions arising where it might be the higher choice.

Let me repeat that, for the nation as with the individual, these high moments must rest on something else. They are the high mountain peaks of the moral life; but detached mountain peaks are impossible,—except as a mirage. They must rest upon the granite foundation of the hills and plateaus below. So these high virtues of non-resistance, magnanimity and self-sacrifice must always rest upon the granite foundation of the masculine virtues of self-affirmation, endurance, heroism, strong conflict with evil. It takes strength to make magnanimity and self-sacrifice possible, if their lesson is not lost. A weak man cannot be magnanimous, since his generosity is mistaken for servile cowardice. After all, the best time to forgive your enemy, for his good and yours, is not when he has his foot on your neck: he is apt to misunderstand and think you are afraid. It is often better to wait until you can get on your feet and face him, man to man, and then if you can forgive him, it is so much the better for you, for him and for all concerned.

Thus there are two opposite lines of error in the moral life. The philosophy of the one is given by Nietzsche, while Tolstoy, in certain extremes of his teaching, represents the other. Nietzsche, I suppose, should be regarded as a symptom, rather than a cause of anything important; but the ancestors of Nietzsche were Goethe and Ibsen, with their splendid gospel of self-realization. Nietzsche, on the contrary, with his contempt for the morality of Christianity as the morality of slaves and weaklings, with his eulogy of the blond brute striding over forgotten multitudes of his weaker fellows to a stultifying isolation apart—Nietzsche is self-realization in the mad-house. It has always seemed to me not without significance that his own life ended there.

On the other hand, when Tolstoy responded to an inquirer that, if he saw a child being attacked by a brutal ruffian, he would not use force to intervene and protect the child: that, too, is non-resistance fit for the insane asylum. One of these is just as far from sane, balanced human morality as the other.

It is a terrible thing to suffer injustice; it is far worse to perpetrate it. If one had to choose between being victim or tyrant, one would always choose to be victim: it is safer for the moral life and there is more recovery afterward. If, however, it is better to suffer injustice than to perpetrate it, better than either is to resist it, fight it and, if possible, overthrow it.

It has been said so many times by extreme pacifists that even sane human beings sometimes take it for granted, that "force never accomplished anything permanent in human history." It is false, and the reasoning by which it is supported involves the most sophistical of fallacies. All depends on who uses the force and the purpose for which it is used. The force employed by tyranny and injustice accomplishes nothing permanent in history. Why? Because tyranny and injustice are in their very nature transient, they are opposed to the moral order of the universe and, in the end, must pass. On the other hand, the force employed on the part of liberty and justice has attained most of the ends of civilization we cherish to-day. The force of the million of mercenaries, collected through Asia and Africa by Darius and Xerxes, to overwhelm a few Greek cities, accomplished nothing permanent in history; but the force of the ten thousand Athenians who fought at Marathon and of the other thousands at Salamis, saved democracy for Europe and made possible the civilization of the Occident. The force employed by King Louis of France to support a tottering throne and continue the exploitation of the people by an idle and selfish aristocratic caste, accomplished nothing permanent in history; but the force of those Frenchmen who marched upon Paris, singing the Marseillaise, made possible the freedom and culture of the last hundred years. The force employed by King George of England, to wring taxes without representation from reluctant colonies, accomplished nothing permanent in history, but the force which, at Bunker Hill and Concord Bridge, "fired the shot heard round the world," achieved the liberty and democracy of the American continent.

It may be freely admitted that all use of force is a confession of failure to find a better way. If you use force in the education of a child, it is such a confession of failure. So is it if force is used in controlling defectives and criminals, or in adjusting the relations of the nations; but note that the failure may be one for which the individual parent, teacher, society, state or nation is in no degree responsible. Force is a tragic weapon—and the ultimate one.

IX

PREPAREDNESS FOR SELF-DEFENSE

Since force is still the weapon of international justice, readiness and willingness to use it for defense, when necessary, is then the first condition of fulfilling the aims and serving the causes for which America stands. In other words, since the relations of the nations are still so largely those of individuals under the conditions of frontier life, as with the honest man on the frontier, so for the self-respecting, peace-loving nation to-day, it is well to carry a gun and know how to shoot.

Carrying a gun is a dangerous practice, for two reasons: it may go off in your pocket; you may get drunk and shoot when you ought not. Those are the only two rational arguments against national preparation for defense, in the present state of the world. Let us see. The gun may go off in your pocket: that is, if a strong armament for defense is built up, there is always danger that it may be used internally, against the people, unjustly. That, indeed, has been one of the curses of Europe for a thousand years. It is a grave danger, but recognizing it is partly forestalling it; moreover, we would better face that danger than one far worse. So with the other menace: you may get drunk and shoot when you ought not. Nations get drunk: they get drunk with pride, arrogance, aggressive ambition, revenge, even with panic terror, and so shoot when they should not. This, also, is a grave danger; but here, as well, recognizing it is part way forestalling it, and this danger, too, we would better face than one far more terrible. Moreover, it is armament for the gratification of aggressive ambition, and under the control of the arbitrary authority of a despotic individual or group, that tends to initiate war, not armament solely to defend the liberties of a people.

Thus, under the conditions cited, it is well to be armed and prepared. If a wolf is at large, if a mad dog is loose, if a madman is abroad with an ax, it is the part of wisdom to have an adequate weapon and be prepared to use it. If the Athenians had not resisted the hordes of Asia, what would have been the history of Europe? If the French had not resisted tyranny and injustice in the Revolution, what would have been the civilization of the last hundred years? If the English colonists had not resisted taxation without representation, what would be the present status of America? If the artisan groups had not united and fought economic exploitation, what would be their life to-day? If Belgium had not resisted Germany, what would be the future of democracy in Europe? Thus, now and after the War, the need is for all necessary armament for self-respecting self-defense and not an atom to gratify aggressive ambition. This does not mean that, once involved in war, the military tactics of democracy should be merely defensive. As has often and wisely been said, in war the best defense is a swift and hard attack.

It is widely argued, however, since our aim is peace and a world-court of justice to settle the disputes among the nations, making general disarmament possible, should not one great nation, fortunately free from the quarrels of Europe, occupying the major portion of a continent, its shores washed by two great oceans, with peaceful friendship on the north and weak anarchy on the south—should not such a nation take the lead, disarm and set an example to mankind? It is a beautiful dream! Would that those who really believe in non-resistance to evil would be logical, and apply it to internal as well as external policy. What is a police force? It is a body of men, trained, employed and paid to use force in resisting evil. If you wish to try out non-resistance, why not let some city apply it? Let Chicago do it: abolish its police force and set the example to the rest of the benighted cities of the country. What would happen? As long as there are criminals in all cities of the land, how they would flock to that fat pasturage. What devastation of property, destruction of life, injury to innocent women and children! Until the best men of Chicago would get together, form a vigilance committee, shoot some of the criminals, hang others, drive the rest out; and Chicago would get back to law and order, with courts of justice and a regular police body, composed of men trained, employed and paid to use force in resisting evil.

The example of Canada and the United States is cited, and a noble example it is: three thousand and more miles of international boundary, with never a shining gun or bristling fortress on the entire frontier. A glorious example, prophetic of what is coming all over the world, perhaps more quickly than we dare hope to-day; but what made it possible? Agreement in advance, and that at a time when one of the parties was too weak to be feared. Canada is getting strong: she has at present four hundred thousand trained men at the front or ready to go. Before the War closes she will have over a half million. Now suppose Canada fortified: we would be compelled to, there would be no other way.

Thus one nation cannot disarm while the others are strongly armed, and among them are those whose autocratic rulers and imperialistic castes are watching for signs of weakness in order to perpetrate international claim-jumping.

It is true that, on the frontier, in the early days, there were individuals who went about unarmed among the gun men, did it successfully, and some of them died peacefully in their beds: Christian ministers—sky-pilots, they were called. Please note, however, that the sky-pilot never had any money. He had no claims to be jumped.

We are not sky-pilots—far from it. As to money: the wealth of the world has been flowing into our coffers in a golden stream, to the embarrassment of our financial institutions, to the exaltation of the cost of living to such a point that, with more money than we ever dreamed of having, we find it more difficult to buy enough to eat and wear. As for claims to be jumped: they are on every hand: Panama Canal, Hawaiian Islands, Philippine Islands, ports of New York and San Francisco, vast reaches of unprotected coast. No, we are not sky-pilots, we cannot claim exemption on that ground.

Suppose, after the War, we attempted to disarm, without the protection of a world court and international police, while the other nations retained war armament. They, the victors and perhaps the defeated, would possess a great army and navy, manned with seasoned veterans, and be burdened with an intolerable debt; for the War has gone too far for any one to be able to pay adequate indemnity. We, rich, young, heedless, sure that no one on earth could ever whip us, chiefly because no one worth while has ever seriously tried: suppose we were completely disarmed. It would require only a little meddling with Mexico or Brazil, and we should have to give up the Monroe Doctrine or fight. Well, perhaps we shall give it up: it has even been suggested in the halls of Congress that we should—to the shame of the suggester, be it said. People do not understand the Monroe Doctrine: they talk of it as if it were a law. It is in no sense a law, but is merely a rather arrogant expression of our desires. We said to the other nations: "We desire that none of you henceforth shall fence in any part of our front or back yard, or the front or back yard of any of our neighbors, dwelling on the North and South American continents." That is the Monroe Doctrine, and that is all that it is: an expression of our wishes. All very well if others choose to respect them, but suppose some one does not? Perhaps, as stated, we may abandon the Monroe Doctrine: that is the easiest way, and the easiest way, for a nation or an individual, is usually the way of damnation. Even so, suppose the nation in question to say, "My national aspirations demand the Panama Canal, the Philippine Islands, or Long Island and the Port of New York." Why not? The Atlantic Ocean is only a mill-pond. It is not half so wide as Lake Erie was fifty years ago, in relation to modern means of transportation and communication. People say, "Do we want to give up our traditional isolation?" They are too late in asking the question: that isolation is irrecoverably gone. That should be now evident even to people dwelling in fatuously fancied security between the Alleghenies and the Rockies. We are inevitably drawn into relation with the rest of mankind. The question is no longer, "Shall we take a part in world problems?", but "What part shall we take?"

The point is, that if, under the circumstances cited, any one wished to do so, we could quickly be driven to such a condition of abject humiliation that we should be compelled to fight. Now suppose, disarmed, we should enter the conflict utterly unprepared? The result would be, hundreds of thousands of young men, going out bravely in obedience to an ideal— untrained and half equipped—to be butchered, a humiliating peace, and an indemnity of many billions to be groaned under for fifty years.

On the other hand, if we were adequately armed for defense, there would be much less temptation to any one to trouble us; and if we were compelled to fight, would it not be better to fight reasonably prepared?

There is a story, going the rounds of the press, about the bandit, Jesse James: telling how, on one occasion, he went to a lonely farm house to commandeer a meal. Entering, he found one woman, a widow, alone and weeping bitterly. He asked her what was the matter, and she replied that, in one hour, the landlord was coming, and if she did not have her mortgage money, she would lose her little farm and home and be out in the world, shelterless. The heart of the bandit was touched. He gave her the money to pay off the mortgage, hid in the brush and held up the landlord on the way back.

Need the moral be pointed? We have been getting the mortgage money. During the first years of the War it rolled in, an ever-increasing golden stream, until we held a mortgage on numerous European nations. We have the mortgage money, but *beware of the way back!*

Thus the agitation, in one nation, for disarmament, unpreparedness and a patched up peace, while the other nations are armed and embittered, not only renders the situation of the one people critically perilous, but actually cripples its power to serve the cause of world peace and humanity. If only the peace-at-any-price people had to pay the price, one would be willing to wait and see what happened; but they never pay it, they take to cover. It is those hundreds of thousands of splendid young men, going out blithely in obedience to duty, to be butchered, it is the millions of women and children, who cannot escape from a devastated area, who pay that price.

Every people in the past that turned to money and mercenaries for defense has gone down. No people ever survived that was unable and unwilling to fight for its liberties and spend, if necessary, the last drop of its blood for the principles it believed.

X

RECONSTRUCTION FROM THE WAR

We have seen how impossible it is to forecast the new world that will follow the War, we know merely that it will be utterly new. Nevertheless, the great tendencies already at work we can partly discern and recognize something of what they promise. It is well to try to see them, that we may be not too unready to welcome the opportunity and accept the burden of the world that is being born in pain.

Peace and prosperity produce a peculiar type of conservatism. People are then relatively free in action and expression, things are going well with them, and they are instinctively inclined to let well enough alone. Thus in thought they tend to a conservative inertia.

On the other hand, in periods of great strain and suffering, as in war time, thought is stimulated, all ordinary views are broken down and the most radical notions are widely disseminated and even taken for granted by those who, shortly before, would have been scandalized by them. Action and certain phases of free speech are, in such a period, much more widely restrained by authority. There is a swift and strong development of social control, urged by necessity.

Thus, in war time, there is the curious paradox of ever widening radicalism in thought, with constantly decreasing freedom in action and expression. When the discrepancy becomes too great, you have the explosion— Revolution. This cause hastened and made more extreme the Russian Revolution, which had been simmering for a century. It has not yet appeared in Germany because of the forty years of successful work in drilling the mind of the German people to march in goose-step; yet the increasing signs of questioning the infallibility of the existing regime and system in Germany give evidence that there, too, the conflict is at work.

With ourselves, the opposition appears, as yet, only in minor degree. Nevertheless, it is here. On the one hand, are the registration, conscription and espionage measures, the effort to control news, the governmental supervision of food supplies, transportation, production and corporation earnings, the war taxes. On the other hand, thought is so stimulated that everything is questioned: our political system, our social institutions— marriage, the family, education. As some one says, "Nothing is radical now." We probably shall escape a sudden revolution, but the conflict must produce profound readjustment in every aspect of our life; for thought and action must come measurably together, since they are related as soul and body.

There are singular eddies in the main current both ways. For instance, the exigencies and sufferings of war produce a reaction toward narrower, orthodox forms of religion and a harsher spirit of nationalism; while in fields of action apart from the struggle, freedom and even license may increase, as in sex-relations. Nevertheless these cross-currents, while they may obscure, do not alter the main tendencies, which move swiftly and increasingly toward the essential conflict.

Even before our actual entrance into the War, its profound influence upon both our thinking and our conduct and institutions was evident. Now that we are in the conflict that influence is multiplied. We are aroused to new seriousness of thought. The frivolity and selfish pleasure-seeking that have marked our life for recent decades are decreasing. We may reasonably hope that the literature of superficial cleverness and smart cynicism, which has been in vogue for the last period, will have had its day, that the perpetrators of such literature will be, measurably speaking, without audience at the conclusion of the War.

The philosophy of complacency, at least, will be at an end, and the world will face with new earnestness the problem of life. This generation will be tired, perhaps exhausted, by the titanic struggle; but youth comes on, fresh and eager, with exhaustless vital energy, and the generations to come will take the heritage and work out the new philosophy. As Nature quickly and quietly covers the worst scars we make in her breast, so Man has a power of recovery, beyond all that we could dream. It is to that we must look, across the time of demoniac destruction.

We may even dare to hope that the next half-century will see a great development of noble literature in our own land. War for liberty, justice and humanity always tends to create such a productive period in literature and the other fine arts. The struggle with Persia was behind the Periclean age in Athens. It was the conflict of England with the overshadowing might of Spain that so vitalized the Elizabethan period. The Revolution was behind the one important school of literature our own country has produced hitherto.

Since this War is waged on a scale far more colossal than any other in human history, and since liberty and democracy are at stake, not only in one land, but throughout the world and for the entire future of humanity, it is reasonable to expect that the stimulation to the creation of art and literature will be far greater than that following any previous struggle. Where the sacrifice for high aims has been greatest, the inspiration should be greatest, as in France. The literature currently produced, as in the books of Loti,

Maeterlinck and Rolland, is scrappy and disappointing, it is true; but that is to be expected when the whole nation is strained to its last energy and gasping for breath, under the titanic struggle, and is no test of what will be. In spite of the destruction of so large a fraction of her manhood, France will surely rise from the ashes of this world conflagration regenerated and reinspired. The pessimism of her late decades will be gone. The literature and other art she will produce will be instinct with new earnestness and exalted vision, and she may excel even her own great past.

We too are awakening. Since the War began, all over the United States, men and women have been thinking more earnestly and have been more willing to listen to the expression of serious thought than ever before for the last quarter century. Now that the hour of sacrifice has struck, this earnestness must greatly deepen. Perhaps we, too, may have our golden age of art.

The same inspiration carries naturally into the religious life. It is true, as we have seen, that there is a cross-current of reversion to narrower orthodoxy, caused by the War. The Gods of War are all national and tribal divinities. While they rule, the face of the God of Humanity is veiled. The Kaiser's possessive attitude toward the Divine is but the extreme case of what War does to the religious life. Even among ourselves the tendency shows in such phenomena as the current popular evangelism—an eloquent, if artfully calculated and vulgarized preaching of the purely personal virtues, with an ignorance that there is a social problem in modern civilization, profound as that displayed by a mediaeval churchman. The evangelist's list of inmates, whom he relegates to the kingdom of the lost, makes the place singularly attractive to the lover of good intellectual society.

Nevertheless, the reversion to narrower creeds but indicates the newly awakened hunger of the religious life. Men who sacrifice live with graver earnestness than those who are carelessly prosperous. Cynicism and pessimism are children of idleness and frivolity, never of heroic sacrifice and nobly accepted pain. These latter foster faith in life and its infinite and eternal meaning. Thus, with all the tragic submerging of our spiritual heritage the War involves, we may hope that it will cause a revival, not of emotional hysteria, but of deepened faith in the spirit, in the supreme worth of life, until at last we may see the dawn of the religion of humanity.

XI

THE WAR AND EDUCATION

Equally far-reaching are the changes the War must produce in our education. Temporarily, our higher institutions will be crippled by the drawing off of the youth of the land for war. This is one of the unfortunate sacrifices such a struggle involves. We must see to it that it is not carried too far. One still hears old men in the South pathetically say, "I missed my education because of the Civil War." Let us strive to keep open our educational institutions and continue all our cultural activities, in spite of the drain and strain of the War. For never was intellectual guidance and leadership more needed than in the present crisis.

The paramount effect of the War on education is, however, in the multiplied demand for efficiency. This is the cry all across the country to-day, and, in the main, it is just. Our education has been too academic, too much molded by tradition. It must be more closely related to life and to the changed conditions of industry and commerce. Each boy and girl, youth and maiden, must leave the school able to take hold somewhere and make a significant contribution to the society of which he or she is an integral part. Vocational training must be greatly increased. The problems of the school must be increasingly practical problems, and thought and judgment must be trained to the solution of those problems. This is all a part of that socialization of democracy which must be achieved if democracy is to survive in the new world following the War.

There is, nevertheless, an element of emotional hysteria in the demand for efficiency and only efficiency. Efficiency is too narrow a standard by which to estimate anything concerning human conduct and character. In the effort to meet and conquer Germany, let us beware of the mistake of Germany. One of the world tragedies of this epoch is the way in which Germany has sacrificed her spiritual heritage, first for economic, then for purely military efficiency. When we recall that spiritual heritage, as previously described, when we think of Schiller, Herder and Goethe, Froebel, Herbart and Richter, Tauler, Luther and Schleiermacher, Kant, Fichte and Schopenhauer, Mozart, Beethoven and Wagner, we stand aghast at the way in which she has plunged it all into the abyss,—for what? Shall it profit a people, more than a man, if it gain the whole world and lose its own soul?

In such a time, then, all of us who believe in the spirit must hold high the torch of humanistic culture. Education is for life and not merely for efficiency. Of what worth is life, if one is only a cog-wheel in the economic machine? It is to save the spiritual heritage of humanity that we are fighting, and it is that heritage that education must bring to every child and youth, if it fulfills its supreme trust. Education for the purposes of autocratic imperialism seeks to make a people a perfect economically productive and militarily aggressive machine. Education for democracy means the development of each individual to the most intelligent, self-directed and governed, unselfish and devoted, sane, balanced and effective humanity.

XII

SOCIALISM AND THE WAR

One of the surprises of the War was the complete breakdown of international socialism. Not only socialists, but those of us who had been thoughtfully watching the movement from without, had come to believe that the measure of consciousness of international brotherhood it had developed in the artisan groups of many lands, would be a powerful lever against war. We were wrong: the superficial international sympathy evaporated like mist under the rays of a revived nationalism. The socialists fell in line, almost as completely as any other group, with the purely nationalist aims in each land.

This must have gratified certain despots; for one cause of the War, not the cause, was undoubtedly the preference on the part of various autocrats, to face an external war rather than the rising tide of democracy within the nation. Temporarily, they have been successful, but surely only for a brief time. The victory of democracy will vastly accelerate the growth of the spirit of brotherhood throughout the world.

The terrible waste of the War must of itself produce a reaction of the people on kings and castes in all lands. The suffering that will follow the War, in the period of economic readjustment, will accentuate this. Surely the *people*, in England, France, America, Italy, Russia, and among the neutral nations, will strive that no such war may come again. Even in Germany, when the people find out what they have paid and why, inevitably they must struggle so to reform their institutions that no ruler or class may again plunge them into such disaster for the selfish benefit or ambitions of that ruler or class. How our hearts have warmed to Liebknecht!

The realignment of nations must work to the same end. War, like politics, makes strange bed-fellows. Germany and Austria, for centuries rivals, and, at times, enemies, we behold united so completely that it is difficult to imagine them disentangled after the War.

France and England, long regarding each other as natural enemies, are fused heart and soul. Strangest of all, we have seen England struggling to win for Russia that prize of Constantinople, which for generations it has been a main object of British diplomacy to keep from Russian grasp. Most impressive of all, has been the new consciousness of unity and common cause among the nations of the earth, and the groups within all nations, standing for democracy.

Thus the tide, checked for a time, will inevitably break forth with renewed force. It is probable that the next fifty years will be a period of great change—even of revolutions, peaceful or otherwise, throughout the earth.

To understand the effect on the whole socialist movement, one must distinguish clearly the two contrasting types of socialism. It is the curse of the orthodox, or Marxian, type of socialism, that it was "made in Germany." Its economic state is modeled directly on the Prussian bureaucratic and paternalistic state. Its dream realized, would mean Prussian efficiency carried to the nth power, in a society of as merciless slavery as that prevailing among the ants and the bees. It is doubtless this characteristic that has made so many bureaucratic or orthodox socialists instinctively Pro-German in sentiment and sympathy during the War.

The contrasting type of socialism is that which is really the full development of democracy, its movement from a narrow individualism to ever wider voluntary co-operation. It moves, not toward government ownership, but toward ownership by the people, of natural monopolies. It means, not the turning over to a bureaucratic government, of plants and instruments of production, but the progressive cooperative ownership of them by the workers themselves. It will end, not in the overthrow of the capitalist regime, but in all workers becoming co-operative capitalists, and all capitalists, productive workers, since no idle rich—or poor, will be tolerated. Such socialism, if it be so called, will depend upon the highest individual initiative, the most voluntary co-operation and will include the individualism which is the cherished boon of democracy. It is significant that those who represent this type of socialism and who think for themselves, are breaking away from the orthodox party, under the courageous leadership and example of John Spargo, in increasing numbers, since our entrance into the War. They are as instinctively American and democratic in sympathy, as those of the opposite type are Pro-German.

Even in the most democratic countries, however, the War has caused a vast increase of the undesirable type of socialism: that is one of its temporary penalties. To carry on such a war successfully, it is necessary to multiply the authority of the central government. That has been the experience of England, now being repeated here. Men, who were *citizens* of a democracy, become, as soldiers, and in part as workers, *subjects* of the government in war. To some extent we are forced to imitate the tendencies we deplore and seek to overthrow in Germany, to be able to meet and defeat Germany.

Even so, the difference is profound. The subordination to the government is, for the people as a whole, voluntary, achieved through laws passed by chosen representatives of the people, and not by the arbitrary will of a kaiser and ruling caste. Thus the freedom, voluntarily relinquished for a time, can be quickly regained when the crisis is past. Subjects will become citizens again, when soldiers return to civil life.

Nevertheless, there will be no return to the old, selfishly individualistic regime. The lesson of organized action will have been learned, and a vast increase of voluntary co-operation, that is, of the socialism that is true democracy may be anticipated as a beneficent result of the War. This will be one of the great compensations for the waste of our heritage, spiritual and material, through the War. *The voluntary socialization of previously individualistic democracy will be the next great forward movement of the human spirit.*

XIII

THE WAR AND FEMINISM

Of all consequences of the War, perhaps none is more significant than its effect upon the position of women. Militarism and feminism are counter currents in the tide of history. All recrudescence of brute force carries the subjugation of women. In the degree to which professional militarism prevails in any society, women are forced into hard industrial activities, despised because fulfilled by women. On the other hand, a group of carefully protected women is held apart as a fine adornment of life. Both ways militarism accentuates the property idea in reference to women: the one type, useful, the other, adorning, property. The one shows in marriage by purchase, the other in the dowry system. It is hard to say which is more dishonoring to women. It would, perhaps, seem preferable and less offensive to be bought as useful, rather than accepted with a money payment, as an adorning but expensive possession, where, as with the automobile, "it is the upkeep that counts." Surely, however, either attitude is degrading enough.

The accentuation, in the present War, of the notion of women as property, is evident in more brutal form in the horrors of rape, in the deliberate and organized use of women as breeders, with the same efficiency with which Germany breeds her swine.

Nevertheless, here, too, strong counter currents are at work. As this is a war of nations, not of armies, it is the whole people that, in each instance, has had to be mobilized and organized. In all the democracies women have voluntarily risen to this need, just as citizens have voluntarily become soldiers. Thus women, by the legion, are working in munition factories, on the farms, in productive plants of every kind, in public service and commerce organizations. The noble way in which women have accepted the double burden has created a wave of reverent admiration throughout the world. Thus where professional militarism tends to despise the industrial activities into which it forces women, war for defense and justice causes reverence for the same socially necessary activities and for the women who so courageously undertake them for the sake of all.

Moreover, the increased freedom of action for women will outlast its temporary cause. Once so admitted to new fields of industrial, business and professional activity, women can never be generally excluded from them again. Thus when the soldiers become citizens, many of the women will remain producers, working beside men under new conditions of equality.

The result, with the general stimulation of radical thinking that the War involves, will be a profound acceleration of the feminist movement throughout, at least, the democracies of the world. Already it is being recognized that all valid principles of democracy apply to women equally with men. Regenerated, if chaotic, Russia takes for granted the farthest reaches of feminism. The regime in England, that bitterly opposed suffrage for women, is now voluntarily granting it before the close of the War.

Thus the victory of the allied nations will mean the fruition of much of the feminism that is a phase of humanism. It will mean freeing women from outgrown custom and tradition, from unjust limitations in industrial, social and political life. It will mean men and women working together, on a plane of moral equality, with free initiative and voluntary co-operation, for the fruition of democracy. Just as that fruition will see the end of idle rich and poor, so there will be no more women slaves or parasites, none regarded or possessed as property, but only free human beings, each self-directed and self-controlled, and responsible for his or her own personality and conduct.

XIV

THE TRANSFORMATION OF DEMOCRACY

The nineteenth century was the period of rapid growth in adhesion to those ideals of democracy for which the War is being fought. It is not so well recognized that during the same hundred years democracy was so transformed as to be to-day a new thing under the sun.

Up to the time of the French and American revolutions democracy rested largely upon certain abstract ideas of human nature. Rousseau could argue that in primitive times men sat down together to form a state, each giving up a part of his natural right to a central authority, and thus justifying it. We now know that nothing of the kind ever happened, that society had undergone a long process of development before men began to think about it at all. We continue to repeat the splendid at all. I refer, of course, to the women of antiquity. Where respectable, these were the head of the household slaves, scarcely removed from the condition of the latter. The few women who did achieve freedom of thought and action, and became the companions of cultivated men—the Aspasias of antiquity—bought their freedom at a sad price.

So Rome is called a republic, and it is true that, during the first half of her long history, freedom gradually broadened down from the patrician class to the plebeian multitude. When Rome reached out, however, to the mastery of the most impressive empire the world has seen, she never dreamed of extending that freedom to the conquered populations. If she did grant Roman citizenship to an occasional community, to enjoy the rights and exercise the privileges of that citizenship, it was necessary to journey to Rome. It was the city and the world: the city ruling the world as subject.

The same principle holds with the republics developing at the close of the middle age, in Italy, in the towns of the Hanseatic League and elsewhere. Always the freedom achieved was for a city, a group or a class, never for all the people. Our dream, on the contrary, is to take all the men and women in the land, ultimately in the world, and help them, through the free and cooperative activity of each with all the rest, on toward life, liberty, happiness, intelligence—all the ends of life that are worth while. If we demand life for ourselves, we ask it only in harmony with the best life for all. We want no special privilege, no benefit apart, bought at the price of the best welfare of humanity. "We," unfortunately, does not yet mean all of us, but it does signify an increasing multitude, rallying to this that is the standard of to-morrow.

A third transformation, at least equally important with these, is in the invention, for it is no less, of representative government. Political thinkers, such as John Fiske, have tried to make us understand what this invention means: we do not yet realize it. The development of representative government is the cause, first of all, of the tremendous expansion of the area over which we apply democracy. Plato, in the *Laws*, limits the size of the ideal state—the one realizable in this world—to 5040 citizens. Why? Well, the exact number has a certain mystical significance, but the main reason is, Plato could not imagine a much larger body of citizens than 5000 meeting together in public assembly and fulfilling the functions of citizenship.

We have extended democracy over a hundred millions of population, dwelling on the larger part of a continent; and if one travels North, South, East, West, to-day, one is impressed that, in spite of unassimilated elements, everywhere men and women are proud, first of all, of being American citizens, and only in subordinate ways devoted to the section or community to which they belong. This has been made possible by the invention and development of representative government.

That is not all: it is representative government that takes the sting out of all the older criticisms of democracy. Plato devotes one of the saddest portions of his *Republic* to showing how in a brief time, democracy must inevitably fall and be replaced by tyranny. With the democracy Plato knew this was true. It was impossible for Athens to protect and make permanent her constitution. She might pass a law declaring the penalty of death on any one proposing a change in the constitution. It did no good. Let some demagogue arise, sure of the suffrage of a majority of the citizens: he could call them into public assembly, cause a repeal of the law, and make any change in the constitution he desired. There was no way to prevent it.

It is the invention and development of representative government that has changed all that. We chafe under the slow-moving character of our democracy—over the time it takes to get laws enacted and the longer time to get them executed. We may well be patient: this slow-moving character of democracy is the other side of its greatest safe-guard. It is because we cannot immediately express in action the popular will and opinion, but must think two, three, many times, working through chosen and responsible representatives of the people, that our democracy is not subject to the perils and criticisms of those of antiquity.

The voice of the people in the day and hour, under the impulse of sudden caprice or passion, is anything but the voice of God: it is much more apt to be the voice of all the powers of darkness. It is common thought, sifted through uncommon thought, that approaches as near the voice of God as we can hope to get in this world. It is not the surface whim of public opinion, it is its *greatest common denominator* that approximates the truth.

It behooves us to remember this at a time when changes are coming with such swiftness. Our life has developed so rapidly that the old political forms proved inadequate to the solution of the new problems. As a practical people, we therefore quickly adopted or invented new forms. Doubtless this is, in the main, right, but we should understand clearly what we are doing.

For instance, one of the great changes, recently inaugurated, is the election of national senators by popular vote. Our forefathers planned that the national upper house should represent a double sifting of popular opinion. We elected state legislatures; they, in turn, chose the national senators: thus these were twice removed from the popular will. It proved easy to corrupt state legislatures; the national senate came to represent too much the moneyed interests; and so, through an amendment to the constitution, we changed the process, and now elect our senators by direct vote of the people. This makes them more immediately representative of the popular will, and perhaps the change was wise; but we should recognize that we have removed one more safe-guard of democracy.

A story, told for a generation, and fixed upon various British statesmen, will illustrate my meaning. The last repetition attributed it to John Burns. On one occasion, while he was a member of Parliament, it is said he was at a tea-party in the West End of London. The hostess, pouring his cup of tea, anxious to make talk and show her deep interest in politics, said, "Mr. Burns, what is the use of the house of Lords anyway?" The statesman, without replying, poured his tea from the cup into the saucer. The hostess, surprised at the breach of etiquette, waited, and then said, "but Mr. Burns, you didn't answer my question." He pointed to the tea, cooling in the saucer: that was the function, to cool the tea of legislation. That was the function intended for our national senate. The trouble was, the tea of legislation often became so stone cold in the process that it was fit only for the political slop-pail, and that was not what we wanted. So we have changed it all, but one more safe-guard of democracy is gone.

So with other reforms, loudly acclaimed, as the initiative and referendum. With the new problems and complications of an extraordinarily developed life, it is doubtless wise that the people should be able to initiate legislation and should have the final word as to what legislation shall stand. On the other hand, if we are not to suffer under a mass of hasty and ill-considered legislation, if laws are to stand, they must always be formulated by a body of trained legislators, and not by the changing whim of popular opinion.

So with the recall, now so widely demanded in many sections of the country. In the old days, our candidates were most obsequious and profuse in promises to their constituents *before* election; but once elected, only too often they turned their backs on their constituents, went merrily their own way, making deals and bargains, in the spirit that "to the victor belong the spoils." Therefore we justly demanded some control of them, after, as before, election: hence the recall. Again the movement is right; but if the fundamentals of democracy are to be permanent, that body of men, concerned with the interpretation of the constitution and the fundamental law of the land, must not be subject to the immediate whim of mob mind, and the power to recall those judges occupied with this task would be a graver danger than advantage. They will make mistakes, at times they will be ultra conservative and servants of special interests, but that is one of the incidental prices we have to pay for the permanence of free institutions. The problem is to keep the basic principles of democracy unchanged, the forms on the surface as fluid and adjustable as possible.

It is these three transformations—the abandonment of the old abstract notions and the testing of democracy by its results, the expansion of its application over the entire population, and the invention and development of representative government—it is these three changes that make our democracy a new order of society, new in its problems, its menaces, its solutions.

XV

DEMOCRACY AND EDUCATION

All just government is a transient device to make ordered progress possible. In the kingdom of heaven there would be no government, for if all human beings saw the best, loved the best and willed the best, the function of government would be at an end. Obviously there is no hope or fear that we shall get into the kingdom of heaven soon, and the necessity for government will exist for an indefinitely long time. Nevertheless, government is due to the imperfection of human nature and, as stated, its aim is ordered progress. Progress without order is anarchy; order without progress is stagnation and death.

It must frankly be admitted, moreover, that democracy is not the shortest road to good government nor to economic efficiency. That we recognize this as a people is proved by the drift of our opinion and of the changes in our lesser institutions. Take, for instance, our city government. A few decades ago our cities were so notoriously misgoverned that they were the scandal of the world. Our boards of aldermen or councilmen, representing ward constituencies, with all sorts of local strings tied to them, were clumsy and unwieldy and easily subject to corruption.

So, about twenty years ago, all across the country went the cry, "Get a good mayor, and give him a free hand." That is the way our great industries are conducted: a wise captain of industry is secured and given full control. Being a practical people, and imagining ourselves to be much more practical than really we are, we said, let us conduct our city business in the same way. Why not? Plato showed long ago that you can get the best government in the shortest time by getting a good tyrant, and giving him a free hand.

There arc just two objections. The first is incidental: it is exceedingly difficult to keep your tyrant good. Arbitrary authority over one's fellows is about the most corrupting influence known to man. No one is great and good enough to be entrusted with it. Responsible power sobers and educates, irresponsible power corrupts. Nevertheless we pay the price of this error and learn the lesson.

The other objection is more significant. It is the effect on the rank and file of the citizenship, for the meaning of democracy is not immediate results in government, but the education of the citizen, and that education can come only by fulfilling the functions of citizenship. Thus it is better to be the free citizen of a democracy, with all the waste and temporary inefficiency democracy involves, than to be the inert slave of the most perfect paternal despotism ever devised by man. Thus the movement away from democratic city government is gravely to be questioned, no matter what economic results it secures.

The same argument applies to more recent changes, as the commission form of city government. As in the previous case, reacting upon the scandalous situation, we said, "Let us choose the three to five best men in the community, and let them run the city's business for us." Nearly every time this change has been made, the result has been an immediate cleaning up of the city government; but why? Chiefly because "a new broom sweeps clean,"—not so much for the reason that it is new, as because you are interested in the instrument. You can get a dirty room remarkably clean with an old broom, if you will sweep hard enough. The cleaning up is due, not primarily to the instrument, but to the hand that wields it.

To speak less figuratively: the cleaning up of the city government with the inauguration of the commission system, came because the change was made by an awakening of the good people of the community. Good people have a habit, however, of going to sleep in an astoundingly short time; but *the gang never sleeps*. Now suppose, while the good people are dozing in semi-somnolence, assured that the new broom will sweep of itself, the gang gets together and elects the three to five worst gangsters in the city to be the commission? Is it not evident that the very added efficiency of the instrument means greater graft and corruption?

Equally the argument applies to the most recent device suggested—the city manager plan. As we have largely taken our schools out of politics, and have a non-partisan educational expert as superintendent, so it is suggested we should conduct our city business. Again, suppose the gang appoints the city manager: he will be an expert in graft, rather than in government.

The moment a people gets to trusting to a device it is headed for danger. There is just one safeguard of democracy, and that is *to keep the good people awake and at the task all the time*. Some instruments are better and some are worse, but the instrument never does the work, it is the hand and brain that wield it.

If there is one field where we could reasonably expect to find pure democracy, it is in our higher educational institutions. In a college or university, where a group of young men and women, and a group of older men and women are gathered apart, out of the severer economic struggle, dedicated to ideal ends: there, surely, we could expect pure democracy in organization and relationship; yet the tendency has been steadily toward autocracy. One can count the fingers of both hands and not cover the list of college and university presidents who have taken office during the last fifteen years, only on condition that they have complete authority over the educational policy of the institution, and often over its financial policy as well. The reason is obvious: we run a railroad efficiently by getting a good president and giving him arbitrary control; why not a university?

There are just the two objections cited above: even in a university, it is difficult to keep your tyrant good. This, again, is the minor objection. The real evil is in the effect upon the rank and file of those governed by the autocrat. There are men in university faculties to-day who say, privately, that if they could get any other opportunity, they would resign to-morrow, for they feel like clerks in a department store, with no opportunity to help determine the educational policy of the institutions of which they are integral parts.

The German university, under all the autocracy and bureaucracy of the German state, is more democratic in its organization than our own. Its faculty is a self-governing body, electing to its own membership. The Rectorship is an honor conferred for the year on some faculty member for superior worth and scholarship. Each member of the faculty may thus feel the self-respect and dignity, resulting from the power and initiative he possesses as a free citizen of the institution.

Let me suggest what would be the ideal democratic organization of a college or university. Why not apply the same division of functions of government that has proved so successful in the state? The board of Trustees is the natural judiciary; the President, the executive. The faculty is the legislative body, with the student body as a sort of lower house, cooperating in enacting the legislation for its own government. Where has such a plan been tried?

If the primary purpose of democracy is thus, not immediate results in government, but the education of the citizen, on the other hand, democracy rests, for its safety and progress, on the ever better education of the citizen. Under the older forms of human society, laws may be passed and executed that are far in advance of public opinion. That cannot be done in a democracy. The law may be a slight step in advance, and so perhaps educate public opinion to its level; but if it goes beyond that step, after the first flurry of interest in the law is past, it remains a dead letter on the statute books—worse than useless, because cultivating that dangerous disrespect for all law, which we have seen growing upon us as a people.

Thus from either side, the problem of democracy is a problem of education. It rests upon education, its aim is education. In a democracy, the supreme function of the state is, not to establish a military system for defense, or a police system for protection, it is not the enforcement of public and private contract: it is to take the children and youth of each generation and develop them into men and women able to fulfill the responsibility and enjoy the opportunity of free citizenship in a free society.

XVI

MENACES OF DEMOCRACY

Since modern democracy is a new thing under the sun, so its menaces are new, or, if old, they take misleadingly new forms. For instance, the greatest danger in the path of our democracy is the world-old evil of selfishness, but it does take surprisingly new form. It is not aggressive selfishness that we have primarily to dread. There are those, it is true, who believe we may soon be endangered by the ambitions of some arrogant leader in the nation. The fear is unwarranted, for our people are still so devoted to the fundamental principles of democracy, that if any leader were to take one clear step toward over-riding the constitution and making himself despot, that step would be his political death-blow. No, we are not yet endangered by the aggressive ambitions of those at the front, but we are in grave danger from the negative selfishness of indifference, shown in its worst form by just those people who imagine they are good because they are respectable, whereas they may be merely good—for nothing.

Plato argued that society could never have patriotism in full measure until the family was abolished. A singular notion that any school boy to-day can readily answer, yet here is the curious situation. Family life, among ourselves, in its better aspects, has reached a higher plane than ever before in any people. More marriages are made on the only decent basts of any marriage. This is the woman's land. Children have their rights and privileges, even to their physical, mental and moral detriment. It is here that men most willingly sacrifice for their families, slaving through the hot summer in the cities, to send wife and children to the seashore or the mountains; yet it is just here that men most readily unhinge their consciences when they turn from private to public life.

Some cynic has said that there is not an American citizen who would not smuggle to please his wife. Of course the statement is not true, but if you have ever crossed the ocean on a transatlantic liner, and watched the devices to which ordinarily decent men—men who would be ashamed to steal your pocket handkerchief or to lie to you as an individual—will resort, in order to lie to the government or steal from the government, you begin to wonder if the cynic was not right. The law, obviously, may be unjust: if so, protest against it and seek to have it changed, but while it is the law, does it not deserve your respectful obedience, unless you would add to the dangerously growing disrespect for all law?

Next to the menace of selfishness is that of ignorance, and this, too, takes confusingly new form. It is not ignorance of scientific fact and law, dangerous as that is, that threatens, but ignorance of what our institutions mean, of what they have cost, of the ideal for which we stand among the nations. The celerity with which, even during the past two decades, the younger generation has abandoned old standards and ideals, is an ominous illustration. It is true:

"New occasions teach new duties, time makes ancient goods uncouth; 'They must upward still, and onward, who would keep abreast of Truth."

Those words of Lowell's are as fully applicable to the present crisis, as to that for which Lowell wrote them; but to give up the past, without knowing that you are letting go, is surely not the part of wisdom.

A third menace shows in that fickleness of temper and false standard of life that cause us to admire the wrong type of leader. Probably one half of all the attacks on men of unusual wealth and success come from other men, who would like to be in the same situation with those they attack, and have failed of their ambition. Part of the attack is sincere, no doubt, but if you assumed that all the abuse heaped upon conspicuous men came from moral conviction, you would utterly misread the situation.

On the other hand, men of moral excellence make us ashamed. Now it takes a rarely magnanimous spirit to be shamed and not resent it. We are apt to feel that, if we can pull another down, we raise ourselves. To realize this, consider the growl of joy that comes from the worse sort of citizen and newspaper when some public leader is caught in a private scandal. As if pulling him down, raised us! We are all tarred with his disgrace. There are, indeed, two ways of stating the ideal of democracy: you can say, "I am just as good as any one else," which in the first place, is not true, and, in the second, would be unlovely of you to express, were it true. You can say, on the contrary, "Every other human being ought to have just as good a chance as I have," which is right; and yet you will hear the ideal of democracy phrased a dozen times the first way, where it is expressed once in the second form.

That democracies are fickle is one of the oldest criticisms upon them. We had thought that we were not subject to that criticism, and in the old days we were not. We had the country debating club and the village lyceum. We were an agricultural people, sober and slow-moving. We had few books, they were good books and we read them many times. We had few newspapers, we knew the men who wrote in them, and when we read an editorial, our mind was actively challenged by the sincere thinking of another mind.

To-day, everywhere, we have moved into the cities. The strength of the country-side is sobriety and slow incubation of the forces of life. Its vice is stupidity. The strength of the city is keen wittedness, versatility, quick response. Its vice is fickleness, morbidity, exhaustion. We have our great blanket sheet newspapers, representing a party, a clique, a financial interest, with writers lending their brains out, for money, to write editorials for causes in which they do not believe. We have the multitude of books, incessantly and hastily produced; we read much, and scarcely think at all. We have got rid of the old "three decker" novel, reduced it to a single volume, and then taken out the climax of the story, publishing it in the corner of the daily newspaper, as the short story of the day, so that he who runs may read. If he is a wise man he will run as fast as he can and not read that stuff at all. We have our ever increasing "movies," with their incessant titillation of the mind with swift passing impressions, as disintegrating to intellectual concentration, as they are injurious to the eyes. The result of it all is an increasing fickleness of temper, so that the same people who shout most loudly when the popular hero goes by, the next week cover his very name with vituperation and abuse, if he offends their slightest whim.

This evil breeds another: fickleness in the people means demagoguery in the leader, inevitably. We have said to our public men—not in words, but by the far more impressive language of our conduct—"get money, power, success, and we will give you more money, power and success, and not ask you how you got them nor what ends you serve in using them." That so many have refused the bribe is to their credit, not ours; we have done what we could to corrupt them.

Finally, we are the most irreverent people in the world. We believe in youth, we scorn age. We have splendid enthusiasm, we do not know what wisdom means. One hears college presidents say—half jokingly, of course—that there is no use appointing a man over thirty to the faculty these days. So one hears Christian ministers, in those denominations where the minister is called by the particular church, say there is no use trying to get another call after one is fifty! Of course, it is not true, but it is true enough to be a serious criticism upon us. For what other vocation is there where the mellowness that comes only from time and long experience, from presiding at weddings and standing beside open graves, sharing the joys and sorrows of innumerable persons, is so indispensable, as in the pastor, the physician of the spirit? Still, we will turn out some wise, shy, mellow old man, just ripened to the point of being the true minister to the souls of others, and replace him with a recent graduate of a theological school, because the latter can talk the language of the higher criticism or whatever else happens to interest us for the moment. Obviously, we pay the price, but think what it indicates of our civilization.

XVII

THE DILEMMA OF DEMOCRACY

We have seen that the gravest menaces of democracy are the faults in mind and character in the multitude. Selfishness, fickleness, ignorance, irreverence in the people, with demagoguery in the leader— these are the menaces of American democracy. How then can the people be trusted, since democracy depends upon trusting them? This is an old indictment, searching to the very heart of democracy. Plato made it of ancient Athens, while, more recently and trenchantly, Ibsen has made it for all modern society.

The argument runs thus: democracy means the rule of the majority. Well, there are more fools than wise men in the world, more ignorant than intelligent. Thus the rule of the majority must mean the rule of the fools over the wise men, of the ignorant over the intelligent. Such is the significant indictment, and we are compelled to admit that our political life is filled with illustrations that would seem to substantiate it. The ward bosses, the demagogues and grafters who are given power by the multitude, one campaign after another, would seem to justify the pessimism of Plato and Ibsen.

Is there not, however, a subtle fallacy in the very phrasing of the indictment? The majority does not "rule": it elects representatives who guide. That is something entirely different. When the worst is said of them those representatives of the people are distinctly above the average of the majorities electing them. Take the roll of our presidents, for instance. With all the corruption and vulgarity of our national politics, that list, from Washington, through such altitudes as Jefferson and Lincoln, to the present occupant of the White House, is superior to any roster of kings or emperors in the history of mankind.

What does this mean? It means that *the hope of democracy is the instinctive power in the breast of common humanity to recognize the highest when it appears*. Were this not true, democracy would be the most hopeless of mistakes, and the sooner we abandoned it, with its vulgarity and waste, the better it would be for us. The instinctive power is there, however: to recognize, not to live, the highest.

How many have followed the example of Socrates, remaining in prison and accepting the hemlock poison for the sake of truth? Yet all who know of him thrill to his sacrifice. Of all who have borne the name, Christian, how many have followed consistently the footsteps of Jesus and obeyed literally and unvaryingly the precepts of the Sermon on the Mount? Of the millions, perhaps ten or twenty individuals—to be generous in our view; but *all the world recognizes him*.

Here, then, is the hope that takes the sting from the indictment of Plato, Ibsen and how many other critics of democracy. Plato said, "Until philosophers are kings, . . . cities will never have rest from their evils,—no, nor the human race, as I believe." Once, perhaps once only, Plato's dream was realized: in that noblest of philosopher emperors, wholly dedicated to the welfare of the world he ruled with autocratic power; yet the soul of Marcus Aurelius was burdened with an impossible task. It is one of the tragic ironies of history that, in this one realization of Plato's lofty dream, the noble emperor could postpone, he could not avert, the colossal doom that threatened the world he ruled. So he wrapped his Roman cloak about him and lay down to sleep, with stoic consciousness that he had done his part in the place where Zeus had put him, but relieved that he might not see the disaster he knew must swiftly come.

How different our dream: it is no illusion of a happy accident of philosopher kings. We want no arbitrary monarchs, wise or brutal: from the noblest of emperors to the butcher of Berlin, we would sweep them all aside, to the ash-heap of outworn tools. Our dream is the awakening and education of the multitude, so that the majority will be able and glad to choose, as its guides, leaders and representatives, the noblest and best. When that day comes, there will be, for the first time in the history of mankind, the dawn of a true *aristocracy* or rule of the best; and it will come through the fulfillment of democracy. A long and troubled path, with many faults and evils meantime? Yes, but not so hopelessly long, when one considers the ages of slow struggle up the mountain and the swiftly multiplying power of education over the mind of all.

XVIII

PATERNALISM VERSUS DEMOCRACY

The contrast between paternalism and democracy in aim and method is thus extreme. Paternalism seeks directly organization, order, production and efficiency, incidentally and occasionally the welfare of the subject population. Democracy seeks directly the highest development of all men and women, their freedom, happiness and culture, in the end it hopes this will give social order, good government and productive power. It is willing, meantime, to sacrifice some measure of order for freedom, of good government for individual initiative, of efficiency for life. Paternalism seeks to achieve its aims, quickly and effectively, through the boss's whip of social control. Democracy works by the slower, but more permanently hopeful path of education, never sacrificing life to material ends. Paternalism ends in a social hierarchy, materially prosperous, but caste-ridden and without soul. Democracy ends in the abolishment of castes, equality of opportunity, with the freest individual initiative and finest flowering of the personal spirit. Which shall it be: God or Mammon, Men or Machines?

There is no doubt that efficiency can be achieved most quickly under a well-wielded boss's whip, but at the sacrifice of initiative and invention. Moreover, remove the whip, and the efficiency quickly goes to pieces. On the other hand, the efficiency achieved by voluntary effort and free cooperation comes much more slowly, but it lasts. Moreover, it develops, hand in hand, with initiative and invention.

The negro, doubtless, has never been so generally efficient as before the civil war, in the South, under the overseer's whip; yet every negro who, to-day, has character enough to save up and buy a mule and an acre of ground, tills it with a consistent and permanent effectiveness of which slave labor is never capable. In the one case, moreover, there is the average economic result, in the other, the gradual development of manhood.

Organize a factory on the feudal lines so prevalent in current industry. Get a strong, dominating superintendent and give him autocratic authority. Quickly he will show results. Always, however, there is the danger of strikes, and if the strong hand falters, the organization disintegrates. On the other hand, let a corporation take its artisans into its confidence, give each a small proportionate share in the annual earnings. Each worker will feel increasingly that the business is his business. He will take pride in his accomplishment. Gradually he will attain efficiency, and work permanently, without oversight, with a consistent earnestness no boss's whip ever attained,

The experience of the National Cash Register Company at Dayton, Ohio, proves this. The experiments of Henry Ford are a step toward the same solution. So, in lesser measure, is the plan of the Steel trust to permit and encourage its employees to purchase annually its stock, somewhat below the current market price, giving a substantial bonus if the stock is held over ten years.

If you wish an illustration on a larger scale, consider the mass formation tactics of the German soldiers, in contrast to the individual courage, initiative and action of the French. There are the two types of efficiency in sheerest contrast, but beyond is always the question of their effect on manhood. France has saved and regenerated her soul; but Germany—?

Further, the breakdown of paternalistically achieved efficiency has been evident in Germany's utter failure to understand the mind of other peoples, particularly of democracies. She had voluminous data, gathered by the most atrociously efficient spy system ever developed, yet she utterly misread the mind of France, England and the United States. The same break-down is evident in Germany's failure in colonization in contrast to England's success.

For offensive war, it must be admitted, the efficiency under the boss's whip will go further. For defensive war, or war for high moral aims, it is desirable that the individual soldier should think for himself, respond to the high appeal. Thus for such warfare the efficiency of voluntary effort and cooperation is superior. An autocracy would better rule its soldiers by a military caste; there can be no excuse for such in a democracy. Thus, the utmost possible fraternization of officers and men is desirable, and social snobbery, the snubbing of officers who come up from the ranks, and other anachronistic survivals, should be stamped out, as utterly foreign to what should be the spirit of the military arm of democracy.

Further, in estimating the two types, one must remember that paternalism may exercise its power in secret and that it accomplishes much in the dark. Democracy, on the other hand, is afflicted and blessed with pitiless publicity. Thus its evils are all exposed, it washes all its dirty linen in public; but the main thing is to get it clean.

When it comes to invention and initiative, as already indicated, democracy has the advantage, immediately, as in the long run. We are the most inventive people on earth, and that quality is a direct result of our democratic individualism. It is a significant fact that most of the startling inventions used in this War were made in America—but *developed and applied in Germany.* There, again, are evident the contrasting results of the two types of social organization. The indefatigably industrious and docile German mind can work out and apply the inventions furnished it, with marvelous persistency and effectiveness, under paternal control. We have the problem of achieving by voluntary effort and cooperation a persistent thoroughness in working out the ideas and inventions that come to us in such abundant measure.

The path of democracy is education.

XIX

THE SOLUTION FOR DEMOCRACY

When we say that the path of democracy is education, we do not mean that there is an easy solution of its problem. There is no patent medicine we can feed the American people and cure it of its diseases. There is no specific for the menaces that threaten. Eternal vigilance and effort are the price, not only of liberty, but of every good of man. Let things alone, and they get bad; to keep them good, we must struggle everlastingly to make them better. Leave the pool of politics unstirred by putting into it ever new individual thought and ideal, and how quickly it becomes a stagnant, ill-smelling pond. Leave a church unvitalized, by ever fresh personal consecration, and how quickly it becomes a dead form, hampering the life of the spirit. Leave a university uninfluenced by ever new earnestness and devotion on the part of student and teacher, and how soon it becomes a scholastic machine, positively oppressing the mind and spirit.

There is a true sense in which the universe exists momentarily by the grace of God. Take light away, and you have darkness. Take darkness away, and you have not necessarily light; you might have chaos. Take health away, and you have disease. Take disease away, and you have not necessarily health; you may have death. Take virtue away, and you have vice. Take vice away, and you have not necessarily virtue; you might have negative respectability. Thus it is the continual affirmation of the good that keeps the heritage of yesterday and takes the step toward to-morrow.

Nevertheless, if there is no easy solution of the problem, there are certain big lines of attack. If we are right in our diagnosis, that the problem of democracy is a problem of education, then our whole system of education, for child, youth and adult, should be reconstructed to focus upon the building of positive and effective moral personality.

American education began as a subsidiary process. Children got organic education in the home, on the farm, in the work shop. They went to school to get certain formal disciplines, to learn to read, write and cipher and to acquire formal grammar. With the moving into the cities, the industrial revolution and the entire transformation of our life, the school has had to take over more and more of the process of organic education. If children fail to get such education in the school, they are apt to miss it altogether.

With this entire change in the meaning of the school, old notions of its purpose still survive. Probably no one is so benighted to-day as to imagine that the chief function of the school is to fill the mind with information; but there are many who still hold to the tradition that the chief purpose of education is to sharpen the intellectual tools of the individual for the sake of his personal success. This notion is a misleading survival, for tools are of value only in terms of the character using them. The same equipment may serve, equally, good or bad ends. Only as education focusses on the development of positive and effective moral character can it aid in solving the problem of democracy.

Need it be added that this does not mean teaching morals and manners to children, thirty minutes a day, three times a week? That is a minor fragment of moral education. It means that all phases of the process— the relation of pupil and teacher, school and home, the government and discipline, the lessons taught in every subject, the environment, the proportioning of the curriculum, of physical, emotional and intellectual culture—all shall be focussed and organized upon the one significant aim of the whole— *character*.

Further, if education is to overcome the menaces and solve the dilemma of democracy, it must be carried beyond childhood and youth and outside the walls of academic institutions. The ever wider education of adult citizenship is indispensable to the progress and safety of democracy. It is one of the glaring illustrations of the inefficiency of our democracy that there are still communities where school boards build school houses with public money, open them five or six hours, five days in the week, and refuse to allow them to be opened any other hour of the day or night, for a civic forum, parents' meeting, public lecture or other activity of adult education; and yet we call ourselves a practical people! Surely, in a democracy, the state is as vitally interested in the education of the adult citizen as of the child.

Herein is the significance of those various extensions of education, developing and spreading so widely to-day. University-extension and Chautauqua movements, civic forums, free lectures to the people by boards of education and public libraries, summer schools, night schools for adults—all are illustrations of this movement, so vital to the progress of democracy. Through these instrumentalities the popular ideal may be elevated, the public mind may be trained to more logical and earnest thought, citizenship may be made more serious and intelligent, and finally a most helpful influence may be exerted on the academic institutions themselves. It is an easily verifiable truth that any academic institution that builds around itself an enclosing scholastic wall, refuses to go outside and serve and learn in the larger world of humanity, in the long run inevitably dies of academic dry rot.

In the endeavor to solve the problem of democracy cannot we do more than we have done hitherto in cultivating reverence for moral leadership—the quality so much needed in democracy at the present hour? This may be achieved through many aspects of education, but especially through contact with noble souls in literature and history. History, above all, is the great opportunity, and, from this point of view, is it not necessary to rewrite our histories: instead of portraying solely statesmen and warriors, to fill them with lofty examples of leadership in all walks of life?

Women as well as men: for surely ideals of both should be fostered. A colleague, interested in this problem, recently took one of the most widely used text-books of American history, and counted the pages on which a woman was mentioned. Of the five hundred pages, there were four: not four pages devoted to women; but four mentioning a woman. What does it mean: that women have contributed less than one part in a hundred and five to the development of American life? Surely no one would think that. What, then, are the reasons for the discrepancy? There are several, but one may be mentioned: men have written the histories, and they have written chiefly of the two fields of action where men have been most important and women least, war and statesmanship. Surely, however, if American history is to reveal the American spirit, exercise the contagion of noble ideals and develop reverence for true moral leadership, it must present types of both manhood and womanhood in all fields of action and endeavor.

One who has stood with Socrates in the common criminal prison in Athens and watched him drink the hemlock poison, saying "No evil can happen to a good man in life or after death," who has heard the oration of Paul on Mars Hill or that of Pericles over the Athenian dead, who has thrilled to the heroism of Joan of Arc and Edith Cavell, the noble service of Elizabeth Fry and Florence Nightingale, the high appeal of Helen Hunt Jackson and Elizabeth Barrett Browning, who has heard Giordano Bruno exclaim as the flames crept up about him, "I die a martyr, and willingly," who has responded to the calm elevation of Marcus Aurelius, the cosmopolitan wisdom of Goethe, the sweet gentleness of Maeterlinck's spirit and the titan dreams of Ibsen, can scarcely fail to appreciate the brotherhood of all men and to learn that reverence for the true moral leader, that dignifies alike giver and recipient.

XX

TRAINING FOR MORAL LEADERSHIP

Since the path of democracy is education, moral leadership is more necessary to it, than in any other form of society; yet there are exceptional obstacles to its development. We speak of "the white light that beats upon a throne": it is nothing compared to the search light played upon every leader of democracy. With our lack of reverence, we delight in pulling to pieces the personalities of those who lead us. Thus it is increasingly difficult to get men of sensitive spirit to pay the price of leadership for democracy.

Is it not possible to do more than we have done, consciously to develop such leadership? Where is it trained? In life, the college and university, the normal school, the schools of law, medicine and theology. Yes, but if not one boy and girl in ten graduates from the high school, surely we want one man and woman in ten to fulfill some measure of moral leadership, and the high school is directly concerned with the task of furnishing such leadership for American democracy.

If that is true, is it not a pity that the high school is so largely dominated from above by the demand of the college upon the entering freshman? It is not to be taken for granted that the particular regimen of studies, best fitting the student to pass the entrance examinations of a college or university, is the best possible for the nine out of ten students, who go directly from the high school into the world, and must fulfill some measure of moral leadership for American democracy. The presumption is to the contrary. College professors are human—some of them. They want students prepared to enter as smoothly as possible into the somewhat artificial curricula of academic studies they have arranged. The Latin professor wishes not to go back and start with the rudiments of his subject, as the professor of mathematics with the beginnings of Algebra and Geometry. The result is they demand of the high school what fits most smoothly into their scheme.

Now if it is not possible to serve equally the needs of both groups, would it not be better to neglect the one tenth of the students, going on to college, even assuming they are the pick of the flock, which they are not always? They have four more years to correct their mistakes and round out their culture. If any one must be subordinated, it would be better to neglect them, and focus upon the needs of the nine out of ten, who go directly from the high school into life and have not another chance; yet there are states in the Union, where it is possible for a committee of the state university at the top to say to every high school teacher in the state, "Conform to our requirements, or leave the state, or get out of the profession." The threat, moreover, has been carried out more than once.

That situation is utterly wrong. We want organization of the educational system, with each unit cooperating with the next higher, but if education is to solve the problem of democracy and furnish moral leadership for American life, we want each unit to be free, first of all, to serve its own constituency to the best of its power. The problem is not serious for the big city high school, with its multiplied elective courses, but for the small rural or town high school, with its limited corps of teachers and its necessarily fixed courses, the burden is onerous indeed.

Is the American college and university doing all that it might do in cultivating moral leadership for American democracy? The last decades have seen an astounding and unparalleled development of higher education in America. In the old days, the college was usually on a denominational foundation. It was supported by the dollars and pennies of earnest religionists who believed that education was necessary to religion and morality. The president was generally a clergyman of the denomination; he taught the ethics course, and all students were required to take it. There was compulsory chapel attendance, and once a day the entire student body gathered together to listen to some moral and religious thought.

Then came the immense expansion of higher education. Courses were multiplied and diversified. Universities were established or endowed by the state. Academies became colleges, and colleges, universities. Institutions were generally secularized. Compulsory chapel attendance was rightly abandoned. Each department served its own interest apart. Until to-day certain of our great universities are not unlike vast intellectual department stores, with each professor calling his goods across the counter, and the president, a sort of superior floorwalker, to see that no one clerk gets too many customers. It is an impressive illustration of what has happened to our higher institutions that, in certain of them, the one regular meeting place of the entire student body in a common interest, is the bleachers by the athletic field. One continues to believe in college athletics, in spite of the frequent absurdities and worse, done in their name; only if the numbers of those playing the game and those exercising only their lungs and throats from the bleachers, were reversed, better all-round athletic education would result. Is it not, however, a trenchant criticism on the situation in our higher education, that so often the one common interest should be in something that is, at least, aside from the main business of the institution?

Moreover, no institution can rightly serve democracy, unless it is itself democratic. Thus the growth of an aristocratic spirit in our colleges and universities is an ominous sign. For instance, it is still true that any boy or girl, with a sound body and a good mind and no family to support, can get a college education. Money is not indispensable: it is possible to work one's way through. Will this always be true? One wonders. It is significant that it is easiest to work your way through college, and keep your self-respect and the respect of your fellows, in the small, meagerly endowed college on the frontier. It is most difficult, with a few exceptions one gladly recognizes, in the great, rich universities of the East. What does that mean?

Straws show the tide: it was announced some time ago by the president of one of our richest and oldest universities that henceforth scholarships in that institution would be given solely on the basis of intellectual scholarship, as tested by examination; and applause went up from the alumni all across the country; yet what does it mean? It means that the boy who has to work on a threshing machine, sell books to an unsuspecting public, or do some other semi-honorable work all summer to get back into college in the Fall, cannot pass those examinations equally with a rich man's son of equal mind, who can take a tutor to the seashore or the mountains and coach up all summer. Thus foundations, established by well-meaning people to help poor boys self-respectingly through college, become intellectual prizes for those who do not need them. That is all wrong.

Take the special student problem. When a college or university is founded, it needs students: they are the life-blood of the institution. Really all that is needed to make a college is a teacher and some students: buildings are not indispensable, but students the school must have. Thus it is apt to keep its bars down and its entrance requirements flexible. Special students, often mature men and women, who are not prepared to pass the freshman examinations, are admitted on the recommendation of heads of d epartments, to special courses they are well fitted to take. Students are admitted freely, and then sifted out afterward, if they prove unworthy of their opportunity: not a bad method, by the way.

A dozen years pass, and the institution wants to become respectable. It is just as with the individual: the man, at first, is absorbed in money-getting, and when he has it, yearns for respectability. Now getting respectable, for a college or university, is called "raising the standard of scholarship." Let this not be misunderstood: painstaking, infinitely laborious, accurate scholarship is a noble aim, well worth the consistent effort of a lifetime; but there are two sides to raising the standard of scholarship. Does an educational institution exist for the sake of its reputation, or to serve its constituency? If it seeks to advance its reputation at the expense of its fullest and best service to those who need its help, is it not recreant to its duty and opportunity?

Well, in the mood cited, the institution raises and standardizes its entrance-requirements and generally excludes special students. One readily sees why: it is much easier to work with the regularly prepared freshman, he fits much more smoothly and comfortably into the machinery of the institution. Many a wise teacher will admit, nevertheless, that the best students he ever taught and the ones whose lives he is proudest of having influenced, were often men and women, thirty, forty, fifty years of age—teachers who suddenly realized that the ruts of their calling had become so deep they could no longer see over them, ministers awakening to the fact that they had given all their store and must get a new supply, business men aware of a call to another field of action— working with a consistent earnestness the average fledgling freshman cannot imagine—he is not old enough; yet generally the tendency is to exclude such students, unless they will go back and do the arduous, and often for them useless, work of preparing to pass the examinations for entrance to the freshman class. That, too, is all wrong.

The American college and university stands to-day at the parting of the ways: this generation will largely determine its future. If the American college and university ever becomes a social club for the sons and daughters of the rich, an institution making it easy for them to secure business and professional opportunity and advancement, to the exclusion of their poorer fellows, it may be as necessary to disestablish the foundations of our great universities, as statesmen in Europe thought it necessary to disestablish the monastic foundations at the close of the middle age. They, too, began as educational institutions. If, on the other hand, the American college and university remains true to its task, if it keeps its doors open and its spirit democratic, if it seeks to render ever larger service to the great public and to develop moral leadership for American democracy, then, indeed, it will go ever forward upon its noble path.

XXI

DEMOCRACY AND SACRIFICE

We have seen the conflict of ideas in the War: the German philosophy that man exists for the state, the contrasting idea of democracy that the state exists for man. We may well ask why any institution should be regarded as sacred, except as it has the adventitious sacredness, coming from time, convention and hoary tradition. It was said long ago that "the Sabbath was made for man and not man for the Sabbath," and the statement may be universalized. Every institution on earth—marriage, the family, education, the church, the state—was made for man and not man for the institution. Humanity must always be the end. Why should we perpetuate any institution that does not serve life? Kant voiced the principle in his second imperative of duty: "Always treat humanity, whether in thine own person or that of any other, as an end withal, and never as a means only." Kant was a Prussian philosopher: one wonders what he would have thought of the "Kanonen-Futter" theory of manhood!

An organization or institution is only a machine, an instrument for a purpose. Thus always it is a means, never an end: its value lies in serving its purpose—the end of human life. So the whole existing order must justify itself. Where it rests on forms of injustice, it must be broken or destroyed, and there is no reason to fear the breaking.

Thus there is no "divine right" of kings. They represent a vested interest, surviving from the past. They must justify themselves by the service of those under them, or pass.

Similarly, there is no divine right of a class or caste, enjoying supremacy or special privilege. It also is a surviving vested interest, that must justify itself, or be swept aside as an incubus.

The same test applies to an empire. It, too, is a vested interest, developed out of conditions prevailing in the past. If it does not justify itself by the largest service of all within it, then it, too, is an anachronistic survival, no longer to be tolerated.

The principle is universal: the institution of private property, the controlling power of captains of industry, the capitalistic system, finally, the state itself, in every form: all are vested interests that may be permitted to continue in the exercise of power only as they prove their superiority to any other form of organization in serving the good of all.

This does not mean that, under democracy, the individual shall fail of sacrifice and the dedication to something higher than himself. That is the glory of life, transfiguring human nature, and without it, life sinks to sordid selfishness. Your life is worth, not what you have, but what you are, and what you are is determined by that to which you dedicate yourself. Is it creature comforts, pleasure, selfish privilege, or the largest life and the fullest service of humanity? What you have is merely the condition, the important question is, what do you do with it? Is it wealth, prosperity: do you sit down comfortably on the fact of it, to secure all the selfish pleasures possible; or do you regard your fortunate circumstances as so much more opportunity and obligation of leadership and service? Is it poverty, even starvation: do you whine and grovel, or stand erect, with shut teeth, andwring heroic manhood from the breast of suffering?

That is why peace can never be an end: it, too, is merely a condition or means. The question is, what do you do with your peace, for peace may mean merely sloth and cowardly ease, where war may mean unselfish heroism. That is what the peace promoters forget. War has its brutalities, and terrible indeed they are: unleashed hate, lust, cruelty and revenge; but war has its heroisms. It calls out the devotion to something higher than the individual from even the commonest of men. To-day all over the earth, ordinary men are quietly going out to probable death or mutilation in its most horrible forms, and going for the sake of an ideal larger than themselves. Women are doing even more than that. For it is not so hard to die, but to send out those you love, dearer than life itself, to almost certain death—that, indeed, is difficult, and women are doing it everywhere with a smile on their lips and choked-back tears.

Peace, on the other hand, has its virtues: the softening and refining of life, gradual development of sympathy, achievement of comfort and beauty; but peace has its vices. In times of peace and prosperity there seems to be no great cause at stake. Of course, always it is there, but we do not see it. We become increasingly absorbed in selfish interests, in the good of our immediate family. Thus petty, time-serving selfishness is the vice peculiarly characteristic of times of peace and prosperity. Consider, for instance, the spirit of France during the closing years of the nineteenth century, and at the present dark, but pregnant, hour of destiny.

Thus the question is not whether you have peace or war, but what you do with your peace or war. It is not whether you are rich or poor, but what you do with your riches or poverty.

Suppose we were able to reconstruct our entire social and industrial world, so that every human being would have plenty to eat, plenty to wear and a comfortable house to live in: would we have the kingdom of heaven? Not necessarily: we might have merely a comfortable, well-decorated pig-sty, if men lived to nothing higher than pigs. "Man cannot live by bread alone," important as bread is, but by dedication to the things of the spirit.

Thus there must ever be the capacity for self-forgetfulness, self-sacrifice, the dedication of life to supreme aims, but that does not mean the dedication of man to the institution. Rather it is the consecration to the welfare of humanity. Man for the State means autocracy and imperialism; Man for Mankind is the soul of democracy. That is the ideal to which we must rise, if democracy is to prove itself worthy to be the form of human society for the great future.

This ideal is realized through many lesser forms and instruments, but always with the same final test. The family, for instance, is one of these lesser forms, and the subordination of the individual to the family unit is just. Thus there is a measure of right in seeking first the interest of the family group; but when this is sought to the end of special privilege and debauching luxury, against the welfare of all, it becomes, as we have seen, an evil.

There is, similarly, a certain justice in the subordination of the individual to the social class or group interest. It is right that artisans should unite in trade unions, that employers should get together in associations for common benefit. One need only contrast the conditions where each workman had to bid in competition against all others, and each manufacturer, the same, to realize the advance made through group union and cooperation. When either group, however, seeks to further its own interest at the expense of the welfare of the whole society, as in securing class legislation, achieving monopolies, holding efficient workers to the level of production of the slowest and least capable of the group, then the class or group spirit becomes an evil that must be fought for the good of all.

It is exactly the same with the nation. Its interest is justly served only in harmony with the welfare of humanity. Any current problem will illustrate the principle, as, for instance, that of immigration.

Certainly the nation has the right to prohibit immigration which produces unassimilated plague-spots and threatens to cause racial deterioration, as in phases of Oriental immigration to the Pacific coast. Similarly, it is right to restrict immigration that would further economic prosperity, at the expense of the manhood of the nation. We must answer the question, whether we want factories or men. It is desirable to have some of both, of course, but when one is to be obtained at the expense of the other, it is manhood that must be the deciding end.

On the other hand, when it comes to refusing a refuge to the poor and oppressed, who are physically and morally acceptable, but lack a small amount of money, or are unable to respond to a literary test, then the welfare of humanity demands the opposite decision. Better give them the fifty dollars—a healthy slave was worth more than that in the old days. So teach them to read and write. The nation, can readily pay the small economic price and accept the incidental difficulties for the sake of the larger end.

Thus the deciding principle must always be the welfare, happiness, growth, intelligence, helpfulness of each individual in harmony with all others. Humanity is incarnatein each man. While, therefore, the individual must dedicate and, at times, sacrifice himself, it is for the sake, not of the state, church or other institution, but for the welfare of all—*Man for Mankind.*

From so many sources the view finds expression that modern life has been "weakened by humanitarianism." If there is truth in the view, we would better take account of it and radically revise our ethical philosophy. If it is false, it is a damning error, the reiteration of which tends to undermine all that has been achieved for the spirit.

An interesting comment on the view is the fact that, in spite of all its horrors, this War has given *no attested instance of arrant cowardice on any front.* Cruelty, lust, brutality, hate: these have appeared in unspeakable guise, but apparently no cowardice or weak timidity; yet the mail clad heroes of ancient wars, who met their adversaries face to face, were subjected to no such strain as the men standing in trenches waiting momentarily death or mutilation from an unseen foe. No, modern life has not lost strong fiber and is capable of supreme heroism.

The old society secured its leadership through *noblesse oblige*—the obligation of nobility. Men of aristocratic family and rank felt that, because they stood above the people, they owed a certain leadership and service, and they gave it, often in abundant measure, but always condescendingly from above.

We have lost "noblesse oblige": we may even be glad it is gone, if we can substitute for it something larger and better. It is not the obligation of nobility, but the obligation of humanity that is the need: to realize that all power is obligation. As you can, you owe; and as you know, you owe. If you have money, it is so much obligation of leadership and service. If you have talent, education, social or political influence, it is all so much obligation of leadership and service.

If, as individuals, we can generally realize that and act upon it, then indeed we may hope to carry to successful completion the experiment of democracy and see our beloved country fulfill the measure of moral leadership to which we believe she is called among the nations of the earth, but fulfilling it not as master over slave, nor as one empire among others, but as a more experienced brother toward others following the same open path.

XXII

THE HOUR OF SACRIFICE

The supreme world crisis is on. We have entered the War in the purest spirit of democracy. We state frankly in advance that we want no indemnity, no extension of territory. We war with no people, except as that people identifies itself with aggressive autocracy and imperialism, imperilling our safety, as of all democracies, and seeking to ride tyrannically and unjustly over the rights and liberties of other peoples. Thus we enter the War solely for the cause of democracy and humanity.

The hour of sacrifice has struck for the American people: will it rise to the test? When one considers the characteristics of our surface life for recent decades—the devotion to money-getting, the rapid increase of senseless and debauching luxury, the reckless frivolity, the unthinking haste and selfish pleasure-seeking—one questions. Underneath, however, is a tremendous latent idealism. We are young, enthusiastic, capable of glorious consecration. Cynical disillusionment is all upon the surface —the cult of the clique of cleverness, uprooted from the soil of common life and the deeps of the eternal verities. Beneath in the great mass of the people is profound faith in life, deep trust in the ideal, belief in the great future of humanity. Democracy will justify itself. We shall rise to the test; but how we need to hear and heed the call!

"Awake America" means Americans awake! For in democracy the individual is the soul. On each person rests the responsibility. Let us accept the bitter burden and meet the supreme test, giving time, money, service, life and those we love better than life, for the sake of the safer, freer, nobler world that is to be. Since we stood apart so long and entered the horrible devastation so late, it is our privilege to do all we can to save the spiritual heritage of humanity, to keep our hearts clean from the corrosive acid of national and racial hatred, to do all in our power to remove it from the breasts of others. Injustice in high places is possible only because there is injustice in the hearts of men. To overthrow tyranny is but the initial step of emancipation: unless the tyrant hate in the heart is dethroned, the external tyrant, in some form of social injustice will surely return. He who conquers hate and the lust for revenge in his own breast is spiritually free and master of the tyrant that wrongs him.

Thus it is our privilege and duty to hate no one; but to hate injustice, greed, tyranny, aggressive selfishness, the wicked ambitions of autocratic imperialism, to resist and help to overthrow them, and so do our part in bringing in the free brotherhood of the nations and peoples in one humanity, that will be the dawn of the longed-for era of universal and permanent peace for mankind.

9 789357 960823